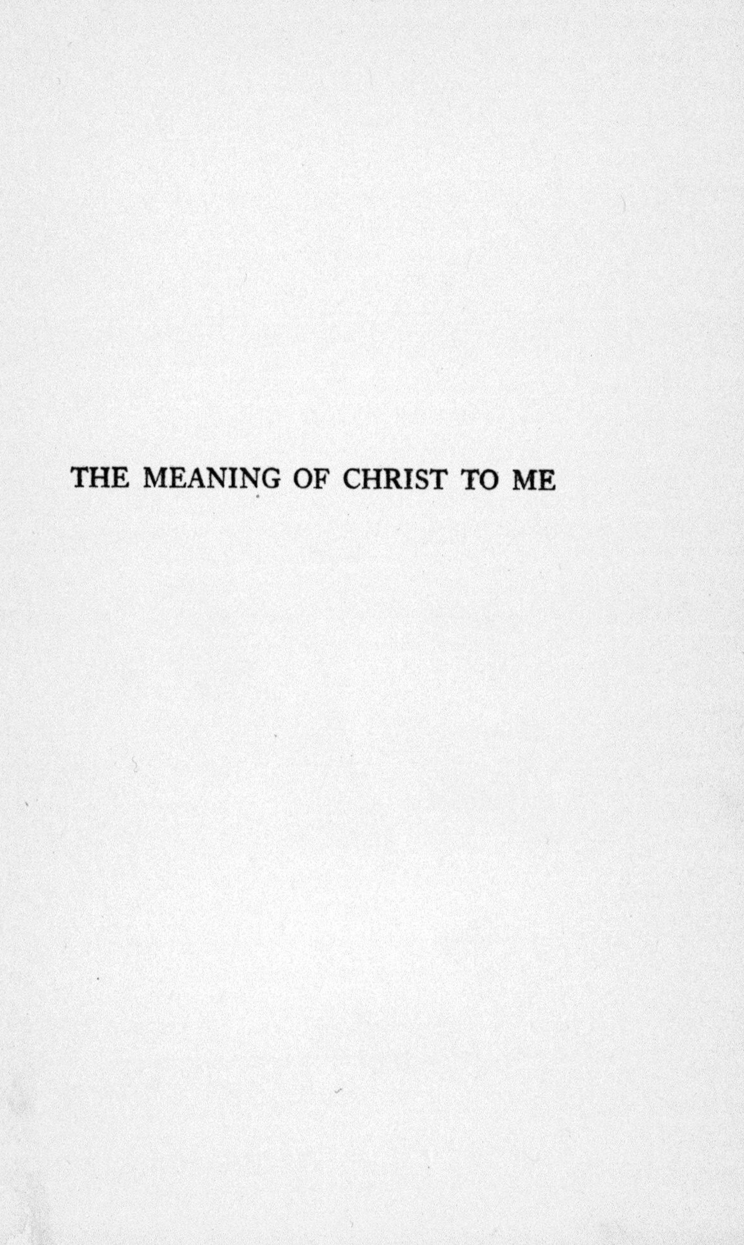

THE MEANING OF CHRIST TO ME

By ROBERT E. SPEER

The Meaning of Christ to Me
Christian Realities
The Finality of Jesus Christ
Some Living Issues
Seeking the Mind of Christ
Race and Race Relations
The Unfinished Task of Foreign Missions
The Gospel and the New World
Some Great Leaders in the World Movements
The Stuff of Manhood
The Principles of Jesus
Studies of the Man Paul
Studies of "The Man Christ Jesus"
John's Gospel
The Deity of Christ
Christianity and the Nations
Sir James Ewing. A Biography
Christian Work in South America
"Re-Thinking Missions" Examined
Owen Crimmins. A Biography
How to Speak Effectively Without Notes

The Meaning of Christ To Me

By

ROBERT E. SPEER

NEW YORK
Fleming H. Revell Company
LONDON AND EDINBURGH

New York: 158 Fifth Avenue
London: 21 Paternoster Square

PREFACE

THE meaning of Christ in human experience is stated in these chapters in personal terms, not without much hesitation but in imitation of the example of those first disciples who went out not to argue for the truth of the Gospel but to bear witness to what it was to them in their own hearts and lives. It cannot be wrong for us today, in our small measure and at our far distance, to seek to follow John: "The life was manifested and we have seen and bear witness and declare" (I John i:2). Very much we do not know, but even we today can say with the man born blind: "One thing I do know." We know Christ and we know that He satisfies.

Four of the six chapters of this book were delivered as the Otts Lectures at Davidson College, North Carolina, in December, 1935. The second and the last were addresses at Student Conferences at Northfield. All have been revised and supplemented.

Their one purpose is to exalt and glorify Jesus Christ, Son of God and Son of Man, our only Saviour, Redeemer, and Lord, and to invite others to seek to follow and serve Him.

R. E. S.

New York, N. Y.

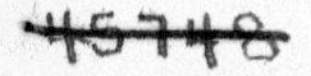

CONTENTS

I

WHAT THE EARTHLY LIFE OF CHRIST MEANS TO ME

THE earthly life of Jesus furnishes an adequate and ever present occupation for one's mind. The mind needs such a sufficient and captivating employment as the remembrance of our Lord's earthly life provides. In his *Life of Gladstone*, Morley says that the wheels of Mr. Gladstone's mind always bit the rails. One wonders whether it was invariably so, whether there was never any wandering that needed to be called in and controlled, such as John Bunyan had to deal with in his thoughts in Bedford gaol. As he writes in the quaint poetical preface to *Pilgrim's Progress:*

> "Nor did I intend but to divert myself in doing this
> From worser thoughts that make me do amiss."

And did not Saint Paul know the reality and urgency of this need both in his own life and in the lives of others? For himself, he says, remembering "the meekness and gentleness of Christ," "though we walk in the flesh, we do not war according to the flesh: for the weapons of our warfare are not of the flesh, but mighty before God to the casting down of strongholds; casting down imaginations, and every high thing that is exalted against the knowledge of God, and bringing every thought into captivity to the obedience of Christ" (II Cor. x:3-5). And he goes straight to the heart of the need of the Philippian Christians with his counsel as to the direction and control of their thoughts: "Finally, brethren, whatsoever things are true, whatsoever things are honourable, whatsoever things are just, whatsoever things are pure, whatsoever things are lovely, whatsoever things are of good report; if there be any virtue, and if there be any praise, think on these things" (Phil. iv:8).

If there was this need of a constraining and absorbing occupation of the mind for John Bunyan and Saint Paul we know all too well the reality of such a need in our own lives. Instead of our minds always biting the rails they are too often roaming abroad in a trackless country or, in changed figures, wool-gathering, vagrant, inconsecutive, adrift without purpose or direction. They need some object on which to fasten, ever present, inexhaustible in its interest and allurement; and for whatever other ends Christ came into the world His human life ideally and adequately meets this need. He is sufficient for all the necessities of our thought.

The highest use of the mind in all of its capacities is to turn it upon the life of Christ. This is the best ministry of memory. So Paul enjoined on the Ephesian Christians, "Remember the words of the Lord Jesus," and so also on his son Timothy, "Remember Jesus Christ." And so Jesus Himself commanded His disciples, "Remember the word that I said unto you;" "These things have I spoken unto you, that when their hour is come, ye may remember them, how that I told you." And those who had been with Jesus did not forget this counsel for themselves or others. Their mission was a mission of remembrance (I Cor. xi:25; Jude 5, 17; II Peter i:12, 13, 15).

One of the most useful and truly Christian movements of our time is the recovered emphasis on the memorizing of the Bible, especially of the four Gospels, the words and deeds of Jesus. In his remarkable work in the mountains of western North Carolina, the Rev. Dumont Clark has developed this plan of what he calls "Scripture Thinking." He describes it in his pamphlet, *Thinking With the Lord:*

"Scripture Thinking is the habitual, thoughtful repeating to oneself, with sincerity and faith, from a store in one's memory, of brief Bible teachings directly applied to life's needs and duties.

"Certain values in Scripture Thinking stand out clearly:

"It is a method so simple that it can readily be used by very young children; and yet it is adapted to all ages and to all conditions of life.

"It fills the mind day by day with many of the great teachings of the Bible and makes them immediately available and effective in all life situations.

"It gives direct and personal knowledge of the Bible as the Book of Life; imparting a higher appreciation of the Bible, and leading the way to a more interested and vital study of the various books, chapters and verses.

"It serves to keep the Master-Teacher Himself in the mind and in the heart, through the constant use of His own words and of other words in His spirit.

"It is a way of prayer; enlightening the meaning and strengthening the use of prayer. Through Scripture Thinking we may actually follow Paul's injunction to 'pray without ceasing.'

"It stimulates Christian thinking, in the choosing of the most suitable Scripture teachings and in their definite application to life situations.

"It is a method that mightily helps those who faithfully use it to achieve a higher standard of conduct and to meet all life's needs and duties more truly in the spirit of Christ."

This is the highest use to which memory can be put, to store it with the pictures, the words, the imagery, the thoughts, the persons and especially the Supreme Person of the four Gospels (John xiv:26; xv:26; xvi:13).

And the noblest faculty of our minds, imagination, was given to us supremely to be used on the earthly life of Jesus. So Mr. Ruskin argues in *Modern Painters:*

"What are the legitimate uses of the imagination; that is to say, of the power of perceiving with the mind things which cannot be perceived by the senses? Its first and noblest use is to enable us to bring sensibly to our sight the things which are recorded as belonging to our future state or invisibly surrounding us in this. It is given us that we may imagine the cloud of witnesses in heaven and earth and sea as if they were present—the souls of the righteous waiting for us; that we may conceive the great army of the inhabitants of heaven, and discover among them those whom we most desire to be with forever; that we may be able to vision forth the ministry of our God beside us, and see the chariots of fire on the mountains that gird us round; but, above all, to call up the scenes and facts in which we are commanded to believe, and be present, as if in the body, at every recorded event of the history of the Redeemer."

The life of Christ is the most proper food for the Christian mind, and the highest function of the human mind is to employ it on the meaning and significance of Christ. As we cannot use our imagination more worthily, as Ruskin holds, so we cannot use any other faculty of understanding and appraisal more nobly than to seek to "apprehend with all the saints what is the breadth and length and height and depth, and to know the love of Christ which passeth knowledge, that ye may be filled unto all the fulness of God" (Eph. iii:18, 19).

This is the first simple meaning and use of the earthly life of Christ. It meets our need for an occupation for our minds at all times, in all places. There can be no loneliness, no sense of emptiness, no vacuity, no wasteful and unprofitable vagrancy with the Christ of the four Gospels available as the ever present, ever satisfying, ever new object of our thoughts, our dreams and desires.

And the earthly life of Jesus meets this need in the fullest and most effective way by furnishing us with an ideal character to contemplate. It does indeed also supply the richest body of thoughts to be found in all literature. Tens of thousands of books have been written on the ideas and words of Jesus and they are still unexhausted because they are inexhaustible. The meaning of Jesus' mission, the living act of the Incarnation and the living deed of the Atonement have been and will be matters of reflection and discussion to the end of time. But behind the truth that He taught and the redemption that He wrought is the Person that He was. It is this Person who commands us, at whom we look. This was the summons of John the Baptist, "Behold the Lamb of God." It was the word of Pilate, saying vastly more than he was aware, "Behold the man." It was the summons of Jesus Himself, "Behold my hands and my feet, that it is I."

For many of us it was the contemplation of this human character of Jesus that either created or fortified against unbelief our conviction of the deity of Christ. There have been multitudes whose faith in this central conviction was established for them beyond all uncertainty by Horace Bushnell's chapter entitled "The Character of Jesus Forbidding His Possible Classification with Men" in Bushnell's great book, *Nature and the Supernatural,* published by Scribners. This is the summary of Bushnell's unsurpassed statement:

"The most conspicuous matter, therefore, in the history

of Jesus is, that what holds true in all our experience of men, is inverted in Him. He grows sacred, peculiar, wonderful, divine, as acquaintance reveals Him. At first He is only a man, as the senses report Him to be; knowledge, observation, familiarity, raise Him into the God-man. He grows pure and perfect, more than mortal in wisdom, a being enveloped in sacred mystery, a friend to be loved in awe—dies into awe, and a sorrow that contains the element of worship! And exactly this appears in the history, without any token of art, or even apparent consciousness that it does appear—appears because it is true. Probably no one of the evangelists ever so much as noticed this remarkable inversion of what holds good respecting men, in the life and character of Jesus. Is this character human, or is it plainly divine?

"We have now sketched some of the principal distinctions of the superhuman character of Jesus. We have seen Him unfolding as a flower, from the germ of a perfect youth; growing up to enter into great scenes and have His part in great trials; harmonious in all with Himself and truth, a miracle of celestial beauty. He is a Lamb in innocence, a God in dignity; revealing an impenitent but faultless piety, such as no mortal ever attempted, such as, to the highest of mortals, is inherently impossible. He advances the most extravagant pretensions, without any show of conceit, or even seeming fault of modesty. He suffers without affectation of composure and without restraint of pride, suffers as no mortal sensibility can, and where, to mortal view, there was no reason for pain at all; giving us not only an example of gentleness and patience in all the small trials of life, but revealing the depths even of the passive virtues of God, in His agony and the patience of His suffering love. He undertakes also a plan, universal in extent, perpetual in time; viz., to unite all nations in a kingdom of righteousness under God; laying His foundations in the hearts of the poor, as no great teacher had ever done before, and yet without creating ever a faction, or stirring one partisan feeling in His followers. In His teaching He is perfectly original, distinct from His age and from all ages; never warped by the expectation of His friends; always in a balance of truth, swayed by no excesses, running to no oppositions or extremes; clear of all superstition, and equally clear of all liberalism; presenting the highest doctrines in the lowest and simplest forms; establishing a pure, universal morality, never before established; and, with all His intense devotion to the truth, never anxious, perceptibly, for the success of His doctrine. Finally, to sum up all in one, He grows more great, and wise, and sacred, the more He is known—needs, in fact, to be known, to have His perfection seen. And this, we say, is Jesus, the Christ; manifestly not human, not of our world—some being who has burst into it, and is not of it. Call Him, for the present, that 'holy thing' and say, 'by this we believe that thou camest from God.'

"Not to say that we are dissatisfied with this sketch would be almost an irreverence of itself, to the subject of it. Who can satisfy himself with anything that he can say of Jesus Christ? We have seen how many pictures of the sacred person of Jesus, by the first masters; but not one, among them all, that did not rebuke the weakness which could dare attempt an impossible subject. So of the character of Jesus. It is necessary, for the holy interest of truth, that we should explore it, as we are best able; but what are human thoughts and human conceptions, on a subject that dwarfs all thought and immediately outgrows whatever is conceived. And yet, for the reason that we have failed, we seem also to have succeeded. For the more impossible it is found to be, to grasp the character and set it forth, the more clearly is it seen to be above our range—a miracle and a mystery.

"Two questions now remain which our argument requires to be answered. And the first is this—did any such character, as this we have been tracing, actually exist? Admitting that the character, whether it be fact or fiction, is such as we have seen it to be, two suppositions are open, either that such a character actually lived, and was possible to be described, because it furnished the matter of the picture, itself; or else, that Jesus, being a merely human character as he lived, was adorned or set off in this manner, by the exaggerations of fancy, and fable, and wild tradition afterward. In the former alternative, we have the insuperable difficulty of believing that any so perfect and glorious character was ever attained to by a mortal. If Christ was a merely natural man, then was He under all the conditions privative, as regards the security of his virtue, that we have discovered in man. He was a new-created being, as such to be perfected in a character of steadfast holiness, only by the experiment of evil and redemption from it. We can believe any miracle, therefore, more easily than that Christ was a man, and yet a perfect character, such as here is given. In the latter alternative, we have four different writers, widely distinguished in their style and mental habit —inferior persons, as regards their accomplishments, and none of them remarkable for gifts of genius—contributing their parts, and coalescing thus in the representation of a character perfectly harmonious with itself and, withal, a character whose ideal no poet had been able to create, no philosopher, by the profoundest effort of thought, to conceive and set forth to the world. What is more, these four writers are, by the supposition, children all of credulity, retailing the absurd gossip and the fabulous stories of an age of marvels, and yet, by some accident, they are found to have conceived and sketched the only perfect character known to mankind. To believe this, requires a more credulous age than these writers ever saw. We fall back then upon our conclusion, and there we rest. Such was the real historic character of Jesus. Thus He lived, and the character is possible to be conceived, because it was actualized in a living example. The only solution is that which is given by Jesus Himself, when he says—'I came forth from the Father, and am come into the world.' "

This valid and incontrovertible view is supplemented in a remarkable German book recently translated into English after a large circulation in Germany, *The Original Jesus,* by Otto Borchert. Bushnell's argument is that the picture of Jesus in the Gospels is authentic because the writers of the Gospels could not have invented it. Borchert's argument is that it is authentic because if these writers had set out to invent a character they would not have invented this one.

It is this glorious character of Jesus that His earthly

life presents as the object of our constant thought and unceasing meditation. But we are sometimes told that this is too small an element of Christian experience to make much of, that St. Paul made little or nothing of it. It is indeed, as we shall be seeing, only a part of the fulness of faith and life in Christ, but it is an essential part, and for many men it has been the only way of approach to the rest. And St. Paul and the other writers of the New Testament certainly did not make little of it. It is what the four Gospels were written to preserve—directly for the purpose, as John says, of leading men on to the fulness of faith—and there are evidences enough of Paul's knowledge and use of the record of Jesus' earthly life and character. As Hausrath says:

"That he knew, in a particular case, to give the historical even to detail is proved by his own statement to the Galatians, that he had so set Jesus before their eyes as the crucified One, that he never believed he would have reason to fear that they turn to another gospel. His knowledge embraces the whole life of Jesus. He mentions His Davidic descent (Rom. i:3, ix:5), and he knows of His baptism and makes an allegorical use of it in his Epistles (Col. ii:11; I Cor. x:2; Rom. vi:3, 4). He knows the preaching of the kingdom of God, and the sending forth of the apostles, and their being furnished with power over the devils (II Cor. xii:12; I Cor. xii:10, 28, 29; Gal. iii:5), and he has so accustomed himself to call them the Twelve, as in the time of Jesus, that he uses this expression even when it was no more applicable (I Cor. xv:5). The poor life of Jesus (Phil. ii:4-8), the spirit of meekness and gentleness that animated it, the self-forgetting, humble, serving love—all this is perfectly present to the apostle (II Cor. v:15; Gal. ii:20; Phil. i:8). He has a more accurate knowledge than the evangelists themselves had of the history of the Passion. At least his narrative of the Lord's Supper in the night of which He was betrayed corrects the differences of the synoptists (I Cor. ix:23); it is not unknown to him that it was the princes of this world, and not the people, that wished the death of Jesus (I Cor. ii:8), and the treachery of Judas (I Cor. xi:23). The reproaches of the Crucified One (Rom. xv:3), His weakness on the cross (II Cor. iii:4), and the nailing to it of the handwriting of the proconsul (Col. ii:14) —all this stands in so living a way before his soul that he can picture it also before the eyes of others. The narrative of the appearances of the Risen One is, in particular, given by him with regard to detail."

And Paul's remembrances, however gained, of the earthly life of Jesus are duplicated in all the New Testament writers. "Consider Jesus," says the writer of the Epistle to the Hebrews, "made perfect through suffering," "who in the days of His flesh, having offered up prayers and supplications with strong crying and tears unto Him that was able to save Him from death, and having been heard for His godly fear, though He was a Son, yet learned obedience by the things which He suffered" (Heb. v:7, 8). "Hereunto were ye called," wrote Peter, "because Christ also suffered for you, leaving you an example, that ye should follow His steps: who did no sin, neither was guile found in His mouth: who, when He was reviled, reviled not again; when He suffered, threatened not; but committed Himself to Him that judgeth righteously: who His own self bare our sins in His body upon the tree, that we, having died unto sins, might live unto righteousness; by whose stripes ye were healed" (I Peter ii:21-24). Years afterwards John recalls the last evening he and his companions had spent with Jesus in His earthly life: "This is His commandment, that we should believe in the name of His Son Jesus Christ, and love one another, as He gave us commandment" (I John iii:23).

It is the fact that the Christian standard has been set

before us in a character which fits it to be universal, as Dean Church said in his famous sermon before Oxford University on "Christ's Example."

"Indeed, it is not easy to see how an example and rule for the world can be, except in the form of a character. For a character, if it is great enough, carries its force far beyond the conditions under which it may have been first disclosed. If shown under one set of circumstances, its lesson can be extended to another, perfectly different: a character is to rules, as the living facts of nature are to the words by which we represent them. It will bear being drawn upon for the application of its truth to new emergencies; it adapts itself with the freedom and elasticity of life, which is very different from the accommodations of theories, to the changes which meet it. When by thought and sympathy we have entered into it, we feel that there are still depths beyond, that we have not exhausted what it has to suggest or teach. We can follow it on, from the known, to what it would be, in the new and strange. It unfolds itself in fact; and we can conceive its doing so in idea, as things round it alter. It is not tied to the limitations and exigencies of its first development; change them, and its action changes too. We see that Character, in which we know that we behold perfect goodness, and which has in fact drawn up the soul of man to heights unknown before,—we see it, as we see all things here, only *in part*. We see it only in a special dispensation or economy; acting, speaking, judging, choosing, only in reference to one set of conditions, according to what the occasion and end called for. It is the supreme and essential goodness; but we see it unfolding itself under the conditions of the supreme humiliation, meeting the demands on it of what the humiliation involved."

"Still, under conditions utterly changed, His goodness is that same very goodness which we saw. And so we can derive from that Character lessons for our state, which is so different from His; and for our imperfection make His perfection the law. And not only so, but we can derive lessons from it for conditions of human life very far removed from those conditions under which His goodness was manifested to us here. The interval is indeed great between those conditions and circumstances, and the state of things amid which we believe that He has called us to run our course. We, instead of being the company of poor men, separate from the world, whom He gathered around Him, and of whom He was one, belong to a varied society of the most complicated order. Functions, gifts, vocations, differ endlessly; we include the extremes of outward fortune, of place and office, and personal cultivation. But under all these different conditions, there is, if we know how to find it, the way in which that perfect goodness would teach us how to feel and how to behave. Literal imitation may be impossible, but it is not impossible to catch its spirit and apply its lessons to altered circumstances. It is true, we have only as it were part of the curve actually traced for us; but the fragment is enough to show him who can learn its real law what, in spaces far removed, is the true line and direction of its prolongation. And so the conformity to the character of Jesus Christ extends, not only to a life like His in its lot and duties, but to one which on earth is called to tasks outwardly as different as can be conceived. In that character, though shown to us in the form of servant, we know that everything is gathered which could make human nature what it ought to be. That perfect goodness was *potentially* all that the sons of men can ever be called to be by the course of that Providence which appoints their lot and the order of their life. His example enfolds them all. It will bear being appealed to for guidance under whatever different circumstances they are called to live: they may learn from it, if we may venture so to speak, how He would have acted in their place, and how He would have His followers to act."[1]

The earthly life of Christ provides an object of thought and offers this to us in a character. It does

---

[1] R. W. Church, *The Gifts of Civilization* (Macmillan).

more than this. It presents this character as normative and imitable.

First, as normative. This conception of the character of Christ is called in question today. No longer, it is said, is "any spoken word of His automatically authoritative for all subsequent ages, or any act a model to be reproduced by all later generations of disciples. . . . Finality is no longer the real word for measuring the value of Jesus." I am quoting from Professor Case's "New Appreciation of Jesus" in his book, *Jesus Through the Centuries*. "His way of life is not necessarily to be our way of life. . . . The new appreciation abandons outright the dogma of normativeness. . . . There are clear evidences in the historical records that He held opinions and entertained attitudes that do not approve themselves to us as suitable for our day. . . . Creative religious living must strive not to imitate but to transcend all past and present standards, not excepting even the example and precepts of Jesus. . . . We prize the injunctions of Jesus as stimuli, but not as ultimate goals. . . . The sacrifice made by Jesus does not stand isolated in its redemptive meaning, but continues to be efficacious only when repeated by His followers in new forms of religious activity under new conditions in modern life. We are not at liberty to substitute the religion that Jesus lived and taught in ancient Palestine for the religion that we must live and teach in our world." [2]

This very clearly was not the view of primitive Christianity. For it, Jesus was the absolute and authoritative norm, and the Apostles and Evangelists conceived that He had so represented Himself. Of the

[2] S. J. Case, *Jesus Through the Centuries*, pp. 351, 353 ff., 365, 374 f. (University of Chicago Press).

mass of evidence in support of this statement it is enough to recall the repeated references in the Gospels to His own self-designation, "The Son of Man." According to all four Gospels this was Jesus' favourite title for Himself. So far as we know, He never used at all some of the titles which we like best and use oftenest, such as Saviour and Redeemer. The ideas back of these names He did indeed approve, but He Himself associated these ideas not with these names but with His favourite title, "The Son of Man." "The Son of Man is come to seek and to save that which is lost." "The Son of Man came to give His life a ransom for many." Others of the titles of which we make use He did Himself use also, "Ye call me Master and Lord, and ye say well, for so I am." "Be ye not called Rabbi, for one is your Master, even Christ." He appears to have discouraged the use of "Messiah," but when the woman at Jacob's well referred to the Messiah's coming, He answered her plainly, "I that speak unto thee am He." He also accepted the title, "the Son of David," and explicitly declared that He was the Son of God. "The hour is coming and now is when the dead shall hear the voice of the Son of God." Indeed, it was for this assertion that He was killed (John xix:7). More often He speaks of Himself simply as the Son. "The Father loveth the Son and hath given all things into His hands." More often still His term for Himself was Lord, but especially, and evidently with special significance, He called Himself "The Son of Man." Thirty-nine times in the Synoptics, connecting parallel passages, He so calls Himself, and ten times in the Gospel of John. Is it not strange that we use so little the title that our Lord seems to have liked best?

Was this an original name with Jesus, or was it borrowed from the Old Testament or from the contemporary Messianic vocabulary? It is perhaps a matter of no great consequence, but each of these views is possible. The phrase is found in the Eighth Psalm, "What is man that thou art mindful of him, or the son of man that thou visitest him?" and in at least three other Psalms and more notably in the book of Daniel. The writer of the Epistle to the Hebrews does not interpret the phrase in the Eighth Psalm as referring to Christ, and it does not seem in the least necessary to find our Lord's use of the title to rest on such quotations or even on the use of the words in Daniel, and still less on the frequent repetition of "son of man," without the article, as the designation of the Prophet Ezekiel in his prophecy. As to the borrowing of the title from current Messianic language, it is clear from the Gospels that Jesus discouraged the use of the Messianic name. He did not wish Himself and His mission to be conceived in terms of current Jewish thought as to the person and work of the Messiah (Matt. xv:20). And the people who heard Him speak gained the idea that the conception of "the Son of Man" was not to be identified with their traditional Messianic notion. "We have heard out of the law," said they, "that Christ abideth forever, and how sayest thou 'the Son of Man must be lifted up'? Who is this Son of Man?" It may be said again that it is of no great consequence whether Jesus originated the title or took it over from the Old Testament, but it is perhaps more sensible and more satisfactory to conceive that it was His own invention. Certainly He put absolutely new meanings into it.

What did the title mean to Jesus? Note His use of it in some of the great statements where it occurs, and consider carefully why He used it instead of some other—Master, Lord, Saviour, or Son of God. "The Son of Man is come to seek and save that which is lost." "The Son of Man hath not where to lay His head." "The Son of Man hath power on earth to forgive sins." "The Son of Man came not to be ministered unto, but to minister." "No man hath ascended into heaven but he that descended out of heaven, even the Son of Man who is in heaven." "And God gave him authority to execute judgment because He is the Son of Man." "Who do men say that I, the Son of Man, am?" "Ye shall see heaven opened and the angels of God ascending and descending upon the Son of Man." "Except ye eat the flesh of the Son of Man and drink His blood, ye have no life in you." "Now is the Son of Man glorified and God is glorified in Him." "Until the Son of Man be risen again from the dead." "The Son of Man shall come in the glory of the Father." "Hereafter shall ye see the Son of Man sitting at the right hand of power and coming in the clouds of heaven."

A little reflection on the significance of these illustrative passages will teach more than the commentaries, but it may be well to summarize the judgment of the commentaries also as to what Jesus meant by "the Son of Man." "Jesus, above all," says Godet, "obeyed the instinct of His love in adopting this designation of His person which expressed His feeling of the perfect homogeneousness of the human family, of which He had made Himself a member. . . . He would designate Himself thus as the normal man, charged with accomplishing the victory of humanity over its own enemy and the enemy of God." "A simple man," says Baur, "to whom cling all the miseries which can be affirmed of any man whatever." "The one," says Holtzmann, "to whom may be applied in the highest degree anything which can be said of all other men . . . the indispensable centre of the Kingdom of God in humanity." "The perfect realization of the idea of man, with the mission of realizing it in humanity," says Wittichen. "The man in whom all the history of humanity must have its end" (Hofmann). "He who realizes the idea of humanity" (Neander). "The universal Messiah" (Bohme). "A true man," says Westcott, "and at the same time the representative of the race in whom are united the virtual powers of the whole of humanity."

And just as the earthly life of Christ presents us with a character normative and authoritative, so it presents also a character that is conceived to be imitable. His normative humanity makes Him for all men and for all time the standard and erects Him as the ideal and example for all mankind. The New Testament rejoiced in this conception. "Be ye imitators of me, even as I also am of Christ," wrote Paul to the Corinthians. "He that saith He abideth in Him," wrote John, "ought himself also to walk even as He walked." "Christ left you an example," wrote Peter, "that ye should follow His steps." But it is true also that we have the evidence of Jesus' Deity in His inimitableness. He was what no one else can ever be. He did what no one else can ever do. The early Church apprehended this and when the Apostles were gone it grew very careful of the dangers in the idea that Christianity was merely the imitation of Jesus. "To 'imitate' or 'be like' Christ," Harnack says, "did not occupy the place one would expect among the ethical counsels of the age. Jesus had spoken of imitating

God and bidden men follow Himself, whilst the relationship of pupil and teacher readily suggested the formula of imitation. But whenever He was recognized as Messiah, as the Son of God, as Saviour and as Judge, the ideas of imitation and likeness had to give way, although the Apostles still continued to urge both in their Epistles, and to hold up the mind, the labours and the sufferings of Jesus as an example." Against any easy humanistic valuation of Jesus as a mere character-pattern or as a character-pattern at all except in the clear recognition of His pattern character as only a fraction of Him, the New Testament Christology, as Harnack goes on to say, stood as a barrier. But this is only to say the more clearly and freely that He who was the unique Son of God became flesh for us that as the true Son of Man He might be the normative and imitable standard for all men everywhere. This was His own word, "I have given you an example that ye should do as I have done to you."

It is to recover the values of the Incarnation that we need to return to the New Testament conception of the imitation of Jesus. With all his limitations Thomas à Kempis has still his lesson for all of us, and Protestant prejudice or indifference that passes him by loses as truly the Christian Gospel as it is lost by any doctrinal defection from Luther or Calvin or Augustine or Tertullian. And it is just here that Christian faith has deeply suffered. As Dr. James Stalker wrote in *Imago Christi:*

"It can hardly be said that evangelical thought has hitherto claimed this subject cordially enough as its own. The evangelical heart, indeed, has always been true to it. I have sometimes even thought that among the causes of the popularity of à Kempis' book not the least potent is its mere name. The Imitation of Christ! The very sound of this phrase goes to the heart of every Christian and sets innumerable things moving and yearning in the soul. There is a summons in it like a ravishing voice calling us up sunny heights. It is the sum of all which in our best moments and in our deepest heart we desire. But, whilst to Christian experience the imitation of Christ has always been inexpressibly precious, it has held, in evangelical preaching and literature, on the whole, only an equivocal position. The Moderatism which in last century nearly extinguished the religion of the country made much of the example of Christ. But it divorced it from His atonement, and urged men to follow Christ's example, without first making them acquainted with Him as the Saviour from sins that are past. The Evangelicals, in opposition to this, made Christ's atonement the burden of their testimony and, when His example was mentioned, were ever ready with, Yes, but His death is more important. Thus it happened that the two parties divided the truth between them, the example of Christ being the doctrine of the one and His atoning death that of the other. In like manner, when Unitarianism seemed for a time, through the high character and splendid eloquence of Channing, to be about to become a power in the world, it derived nearly all the attractiveness it ever possessed from the eulogies in which its preaching abounded of the pure, lofty and self-sacrificing humanity of Christ. The evangelical Church answered with demonstrations of His divinity, scriptural and irresistibly logical no doubt, but not always very captivating. And thus a division was again allowed to take place, the humanity of Christ falling to the one party as its share and His divinity to the other. It is time to object to these divisions. Both halves of the truth are ours, and we claim the whole of it. The death of Christ is ours, and we rest in it our hopes of acceptance with God in time and in eternity. This is what we begin with; but we do not end with it. We will go on from His death to His life and, with the love begotten of being redeemed, try to reproduce that life in our own. In the same way, whilst glorying in His divinity, we will allow none to rob us of the attraction and the example of His humanity; for, indeed, the perfection of His humanity, with what this implies as to the value of His testimony about Himself, is the strongest bulwark of our faith that He was more than man" (*Imago Christi*, pp. 31-33).

And as we recall the earthly life of Jesus we are among those of whom Stalker speaks in the introduction to his suggestive book, so beautifully true: "I am persuaded that there are many at present in all the churches who are turning earnest eyes to the Example of Christ, and who desire an account, derived directly from the records, of how He lived this earthly life which we are living now. They have awakened to the value and solemnity of time, and feel that the one thing needful is to fill our few and swiftly passing years with a life large and useful and ever more abundant. But it must be a life like Christ's, for His was the best; and any life, however filled with excitement or success, of which He disapproved, would not seem to them worth living" (*Imago Christi*, pp. 9, 10).

And not only does the earthly life of Christ provide this adorable figure of a perfect normative and imitable character, but it also reveals one who is normative and imitable just at the points of our deepest and most conscious moral need. Three particulars will suffice.

1. In the matter of forgiveness. In this regard Jesus Christ in His earthly life stands out as the most glorious personality in history. He taught a doctrine of unlimited forgiveness.

"Then came Peter, and said to Him, Lord, how oft shall my brother sin against me, and I forgive him? until seven times? Jesus saith unto him, I say not unto thee, until seven times; but, until seventy times seven. Therefore is the kingdom of heaven likened unto a certain king, who would make a reckoning with his servants. And when he had begun to reckon, one was brought unto him, that owed him ten thousand talents. But forasmuch as he had not wherewith to pay, his lord commanded him to be sold, and his wife, and children, and all that he had, and payment to be made. The servant therefore fell down and worshipped him, saying, Lord, have patience with me, and I will pay thee all. And the lord of that servant, being moved with compassion, released him, and forgave him the debt. But that servant went out, and found one of his fellow-servants, who owed him a hundred shillings: and he laid hold on him, and took him by the throat, saying, pay what thou owest. So his fellow-servant fell down and besought him, saying, have patience with me, and I will pay thee. And he would not: but went and cast him into prison, till he should pay that which was due. So when his fellow-servants saw what was done, they were exceeding sorry, and came and told unto their lord all that was done. Then his lord called him unto him, and saith to him, Thou wicked servant, I forgave thee all that debt, because thou besoughtest me: shouldest not thou also have had mercy on thy fellow-servant, even as I had mercy on thee? And his lord was wroth, and delivered him to the tormentors, till he should pay all that was due. So shall also my heavenly Father do unto you, if ye forgive not every one his brother from your hearts" (Matt. xviii:21-35).

And this doctrine, repeated again and again, He exemplified. He declared forgiveness of sin to men, to the horror of the Pharisees (Mark ii:7). He prayed for the forgiveness of His murderers (Luke xxiii:34). In Him men saw the fulfilment of the highest ideal of which His nation had ever been able to conceive: "Surely He hath borne our griefs, and carried our sorrows; yet we did esteem Him stricken, smitten of God, and afflicted. But He was wounded for our transgressions, He was bruised for our iniquities; the chastisement of our peace was upon Him; and with His stripes we are healed. All we like sheep have gone astray; we have turned every one to his own way; and Jehovah hath laid on Him the iniquity of us all. He was oppressed, yet when He was afflicted He opened not His mouth; as a lamb that is led to the slaughter, and as a sheep before its shearers is dumb, so He opened not His mouth" (Isa. liii:4-7).

The early Church saw in the forgiveness of Christ the law of its own life. "And be ye kind one to another, tenderhearted, forgiving each other, even as God also in Christ forgave you" (Eph. iv:32).

Nowhere do we more need today the influence on our own lives of the ideal of the earthly life of Christ than in this matter of forgiveness. Here is where we are breaking down in human relations inside and outside of the Christian Church. Jude's admonition to contend earnestly for the faith has been carried to limits of bitterness and strife and division at which, we may believe, he would be aghast. What we need is the uptearing, upheaving, revolutionizing influence on our lives of the Christ-like principle of forgiveness. Horace Bushnell once wrote to a correspondent these great and penetrating words, "Nothing does God require more explicitly than a clean forgiveness. Your provocations are multiplied and aggravated. The rasp that is drawn across your sensibilities without respite for successive years, is rough and sharp enough to require the concentration of all the Jobs in Christendom. Be not dismayed; only believe. Great trials make great saints. Deserts and stone pillows prepare for an open heaven and an angel-crowded ladder. But you are indeed sorely probed, and from the depths of my soul I pity you. If this is any comfort to you, let down your bucket to the end of your chain, with the assurance that what is deepest and most tender in me is open to your dip. But your victory rests with yourself. Kinghood over the vast territory of self must be, in order to a genuine forgiveness. To tear yourself from yourself, to double yourself up and thrust yourself under your heels, and make a general smash of yourself, and be all the more truly yourself for this mauling and self-annihilation—this is the work before you, and a mighty work it is. To accomplish this we must be close enough to Immanuel to feel the beating of His heart. By the time you are through your struggle you will be a good fit to occupy a seat with Christ on His throne. Kings alone can truly forgive, as kings alone can reign. You know the import of the Cross. Set your heart like a flint against every suggestion that cheapens the blood of the dear, great Lamb, and you will as surely get the meaning of Christ crucified, as that He left His life in the world."

2. In the matter of prayer. If ever there was a human life which could have dispensed with prayer it was the earthly life of Jesus. For what did He need to pray? For guidance? He knew. "I know whence I came and whither I go." For obedience? "I do always the things that please my Father." For companionship? "The Father hath not left me alone. I and the Father are one." And yet the chief occupation of His life was not activity but prayer. One of the amazing features of the record of Jesus' earthly life is the slight volume of its action. All that is reported of His work and deeds could have been compressed in

a few weeks of time. The great activity, of which only suggestions and no record could be given, was prayer. And His own practice issued in counsel: "Pray for them that despitefully use you and persecute you." "Pray to thy Father which heareth in secret." "Pray the Lord of the harvest to send forth labourers." "Watch and pray that ye enter not into temptation." "Therefore I say unto you, all things whatsoever ye pray and ask for, believe that ye receive them, and ye shall have them. And whensoever ye stand praying, forgive, if ye have aught against any one; that your Father also who is in heaven may forgive you your trespasses" (Mark xi:24, 25). He taught men a prayer which we call "The Lord's Prayer," and He taught them "that men ought always to pray and not to faint" (Luke xi:18). The meaning of the earthly life of Jesus is a school of prayer and an invitation to enter this school.

3. In the matter of the personalism and spiritual immediacy of His way of life and influence. He did not make use of or rely upon any of our customary human resources or dependencies, money, power, organization. He simply made good persons. He did indeed, in spite of what is said to the contrary, set forth great moral and spiritual and social and even economic principles, but He did not embody them in statutes or institutions. He worked with persons, making good men and women. The world, He said, is a great field to be cultivated, and "He that soweth the good seed is the Son of Man, and the good seed, they are the sons of the Kingdom." And these new-created and creative personalities He chose not from the great and influential, but from the common people and the poor. As Troeltsch has said, "Jesus did not

organize a church. He simply asked for helpers who would spread the message by preaching; these assistants were to be men who would leave all and sacrifice everything for His sake and for the cause." And Jesus wrote nothing. That could be left to others. He was and did what the world has been thinking and writing about ever since. He was both the illustration and the refutation of the view of history proposed by J. B. S. Haldane (*Harper's Magazine*, Sept., 1930, "Is History a Fraud?").

Let us go on now a step further in our thought of the uses of the remembrance and the imitability of Jesus' earthly life. The method of this imitability is reasonable and right. It is outward, conscious and voluntary. So John described it, combining the inward and the outward, "He that saith he abideth in Him ought himself also to walk even as He walked." And Jesus Himself taught the disciples this elementary lesson, "If I then your Lord and Master have washed your feet, ye also ought to wash one another's feet." "What would Jesus do?" asked Charles M. Sheldon in his famous book. *In His Steps* has been a natural prescription. It was thus that Fleeming Jenkins counselled Robert Louis Stevenson. "Once," says Stewart in his *Life of Stevenson*, "when Stevenson consulted him on a point of conduct his answer was, 'How do you suppose Christ would advise you?' Stevenson admitted he would not counsel anything wicked or cowardly. 'No,' said Jenkins decisively, 'nor anything amusing?' " And Dean Briggs of Harvard followed the method in regard to his mother. "I do not believe," he said, "any other man ever stood in quite the same relation to his mother. While she lived I turned to her in every kind of perplexity; and since her death

I have continued to do so, not in melodramatic, sentimental fashion, but continually in the course of the day's work. Whenever I am confronted with a baffling problem I find myself asking what her wisdom would have led her to regard as best." [3]

But the method of imitation provided by Jesus was not this outward, objective, will-imposed method. It was an inward, invisible, in a true sense automatic, process. "Henceforth I call you not servants; for the servant knoweth not what his lord doeth: but I have called you friends; for all things that I have heard of my Father I have made known unto you." Paul, who called his friends to join him in the imitation of Jesus, knew this deeper secret. "We have the mind of Christ," he tells the Corinthians and he exhorts the Philippians, "Let this mind be in you which was also in Christ Jesus." And the writer of the Epistle to the Hebrews recalls the great promise given in the old ritual and outer ceremonial, of a better day to come, "I will put my laws into their mind and on their heart also will I write them." This is the method of Christian guidance. Christ within us makes us Christ-like. We walk in His ways because His mind has become our mind. Dr. Henry Clay Trumbull used to tell of an old farmer near his boyhood home in Stonington, Connecticut, whose sons one by one had left the home farm, barely able to sustain those who remained, until it came the time of the youngest boy to follow his brothers. On the Sunday evening before the boy was to leave, the old father said to him, "John, you're going away tomorrow and it will be a long time before we see you again. I'd like to have one last talk with you before you go." So the old man and the boy went out

[3] Rollo W. Brown, *Dean Briggs*, p. 34 (Harpers).

together through the flower-garden in front of the house, across the meadows to the brook, past the swimming hole which the boy and his brothers had made, through the wood lot and back by the fields to the vegetable garden behind the house. All the memories of his boyhood came back over the lad's mind and heart. And all the while the father had said never a word. He well knew, however, what thoughts were in the boy's mind. At last as they stood at the garden gate just before going into the house again, the old man slipped his arm over the boy's shoulder and said simply, "John, I've got only one last word to say to you. Allus do as you have a mind to." That was enough. Of what use would any new counsel have been? If truth had not been wrought into the lad in the twenty years gone, what hope could there be of any last hour admonition? And what need was there? The boy had learned at his mother's knee and from his father's life the mind of Christ. All that he needed now was to follow that mind, to do not as others might have a mind for him, but as he had a mind, even the mind of Christ, for himself.

And lastly and supremely over all else we are called by the earthly life of Christ to His spiritual adjustment toward God. There was indeed just here something unique and inimitable in Jesus. His being, as Dr. George A. Gordon used to say, was grounded in God in a way absolutely solitary. But nevertheless He walked among men as a man, and "we have not a high priest that cannot be touched with the feeling of our infirmities; but one that hath been in all points tempted like as we are, yet without sin. Let us therefore draw near with boldness unto the throne of grace, that we may receive mercy, and may find grace to help us in time of need" (Heb. iv:15, 16). And in nothing does He summon us more gloriously than in this possibility and duty of perfect readjustment of filial relationship to God. It was perfect with Him. God spoke of Him as His beloved Son in whom God Himself was well pleased, and Jesus made three great declarations which are, alike, our despair and our supreme hope:

"I can of Myself do nothing: as I hear, I judge: and My judgment is righteous; because I seek not Mine own will, but the will of Him that sent Me" (John v:30). "Jesus answered and said unto them, Even if I bear witness of Myself, My witness is true; for I know whence I came, and whither I go; but ye know not whence I come, or whither I go" (John viii:14). "Yea and if I judge, My judgment is true; for I am not alone, but I and the Father that sent Me" (John viii:16).

John puts all this wonder of Jesus' perfect adjustment toward God in one remarkable phrase in the prologue of his Gospel, "The Word was with God," literally "The Word was toward God." The face of Jesus was ever directed to the face of God. He saw things not in themselves, their own fragmentariness, inadequacy, and misrepresentativeness, but in the face of God, as God saw them. "Mine hour is not yet come," He said. How did He know? Not from looking at time, but from looking at the Timeless One. "Consider the times," wrote Ignatius. "Look to Him who is above time." All Jesus' earthly life was lived as to God and before God and in God. "But Jesus answered them, My Father worketh even until now, and I work." "Jesus therefore said, when ye have lifted up the Son of man then shall ye know that I am He, and that I do nothing of Myself, but as the Father taught Me, I speak these things." "I speak the things which I have seen with My Father: and ye also do the things which ye heard from your father." "No one taketh it away from Me, but I lay it down of Myself. I have power to lay it down, and I have power to take it again. This commandment received I from My Father." "Jesus answered them, I told you, and ye believe not: the works that I do in My Father's name, these bear witness of Me." "Jesus answered them, Many good works have I showed you from the Father; for which of those works do ye stone Me?" "Believest thou not that I am in the Father, and the Father in Me? The words that I say unto you I speak not from Myself: but the Father abiding in Me doeth His works." "No longer do I call you servants; for the servant knoweth not what his lord doeth: but I have called you friends; for all things that I have heard from My Father I have made known unto you" (John v:17; viii:28, 38; x:13, 25, 32; xiv:10; xv:15).

But is this for us? Or are these footsteps forbidden to us, of the Son of Man who was Son of God? Once again what did He Himself say? "That ye may be sons of your Father who is in heaven: for He maketh His sun to rise on the evil and the good, and sendeth rain on the just and the unjust." "Ye therefore shall be perfect, as your heavenly Father is perfect." "Be not therefore like unto them: for your Father knoweth what things ye have need of, before ye ask Him." "And call no man your father on the earth: for one is your Father, even He who is in heaven." "Fear not, little flock; for it is your Father's good pleasure to give you the kingdom." "Jesus saith to her, touch Me not; for I am not yet ascended unto the Father: but go unto My brethren and say to them, I ascend unto My Father and your Father, and My God and your God." "And ye also bear witness, because ye have been with Me from the beginning" (Matt. v:45, 48; vi:8; xxiii:9; Luke xii:32; John xx:17; xv:27).

There is a remarkable poem of Browning's, entitled "An Epistle Containing the Strange Medical Experience of Karshish, the Arab Physician." It purports to be a letter from a wandering Arab doctor to his old master in Egypt describing a strange case which Karshish has met in Palestine:

"'Tis but a case of mania—subinduced
By epilepsy, at the turning-point
Of trance prolonged unduly some three days:
When, by the exhibition of some drug
Or spell, exorcization, stroke of art
Unknown to me and which 'twere well to know,
The evil thing outbreaking all at once
Left the man whole and sound of body indeed,—
But, flinging (so to speak) life's gates too wide,
Making a clear house of it too suddenly,
The first conceit that entered might inscribe
Whatever it was minded on the wall
So plainly at that vantage, as it were,
(First come, first served) that nothing subsequent
Attaineth to erase those fancy-scrawls
The just-returned and new-established soul
Hath gotten now so thoroughly by heart
That henceforth she will read or these or none.
And first—the man's own firm conviction rests
That he was dead (in fact they buried him)
—That he was dead and then restored to life
By a Nazarene physician of his tribe:
—Sayeth, the same bade 'Rise,' and he did rise."

And Karshish proceeds to describe this strange case of Lazarus, of one who was living this earthly life by the standards and measurements of that other life of which he had seen a glimpse and from which he had returned:

"This grown man eyes the world now like a child.
Some elders of his tribe, I should premise,
Led in their friend, obedient as a sheep,
To bear my inquisition. While they spoke,
Now sharply, now with sorrow,—told the case,—
He listened not except I spoke to him,
But folded his two hands and let them talk,
Watching the flies that buzzed: and yet no fool.
And that's a sample how his years must go.
Look, if a beggar, in fixed middle-life,
Should find a treasure,—can he use the same
With straitened habits and with tastes starved small,
And take at once to his impoverished brain
The sudden element that changes things,
That sets the undreamed-of rapture at his hand
And puts the cheap old joy in the scorned dust?
Is he not such an one as moves to mirth—
Warily parsimonious, when no need,
Wasteful as drunkenness at undue times?
All prudent counsel as to what befits
The golden mean, is lost on such an one:
The man's fantastic will is the man's law.
So here—we call the treasure knowledge, say,
Increased beyond the fleshly faculty—
Heaven opened to a soul while yet on earth,
Earth forced on a soul's use while seeing heaven:
The man is witless of the size, the sum,
The value in proportion of all things,
Or whether it be little or be much.
Discourse to him of prodigious armaments
Assembled to besiege his city now,
And of the passing of a mule with gourds—
'Tis one! Then take it on the other side,
Speak of some trifling fact,—he will gaze rapt
With stupor at its very littleness,
(Far as I see) as if in that indeed
He caught prodigious import, whole results;

And so will turn to us the bystanders
In ever the same stupor (note this point)
That we too see not with his opened eyes.
Wonder and doubt come wrongly into play,
Preposterously, at cross purposes.
Should his child sicken unto death,—why, look
For scarce abatement of his cheerfulness,
Or pretermission of the daily craft!
While a word, gesture, glance from that same child
At play or in the school or laid asleep,
Will startle him to an agony of fear,
Exasperation, just as like. Demand
The reason why—' 'tis but a word,' object—
'A gesture'—he regards thee as our lord
Who lived there in the pyramid alone,
Looked at us (dost thou mind?) when, being young,
We both would unadvisedly recite
Some charm's beginning, from that book of his,
Able to bid the sun throb wide and burst
All into stars, as suns grown old are wont.
Thou and the child have each a veil alike
Thrown o'er your heads, from under which ye both
Stretch your blind hands and trifle with a match
Over a mine of Greek fire, did ye know!
He holds on firmly to some thread of life—
(It is the life to lead perforcedly)
Which runs across some vast distracting orb
Of glory on either side that meagre thread,
Which, conscious of, he must not enter yet—
The spiritual life around the earthly life:
The law of that is known to him as this,
His heart and brain move there, his feet stay here."

And Karshish, half ashamed, reports Lazarus' account of Jesus, and rejects it and yet—and yet the doubt comes back to meet his doubts:

"The very God! think, Abib; dost thou think?
So, the All-Great, were the All-Loving too—
So, through the thunder comes a human voice

> Saying, 'O heart I made, a heart beats here!
> Face, my hands fashioned, see it in myself!
> Thou hast no power nor mayst conceive of mine,
> But love I gave thee, with myself to love,
> And thou must love me who have died for thee!' "

As Jesus in His earthly life lived the heavenly life, and Lazarus after Him, in his measure, so we in our measure too. This was Paul's appeal to the Colossian Christians: "Set your mind on the things that are above, not on the things that are upon the earth." To the end that this might be a possibility for us Jesus Christ lived in the flesh one true earthly life that, living over again that earthly life of His, we might learn how to enter even now and live here in this present world His eternal and heavenly life.

II

WHAT THE PERSON OF CHRIST MEANS TO ME

CHRISTIANITY is the only one of the great religions of the world which calls itself by the name of its founder. Other great religions are named after their founders by us. They were not so named by their own adherents. This is not a mere accident; it is a fact of the deepest significance. To be sure, the name Christian was given originally by enemies, but it was given by them because, from without, they had already discerned the essential and distinguishing character of the new religion, and had been impressed by the inseparable connection which, they saw, existed between it and its founder Jesus Christ. The disciples of the new religion presently accepted the name as the most appropriate name possible for them and their faith. They themselves were aware that the relationship in which they stood to Jesus Christ was the central and fundamental thing in their religion. So long as He had been on earth their religion had consisted in personally following Him, in finding their fellowship in His company, in drawing their nourishment from His words, in coming to understand His Person and His Mission, and in resting their hearts on the peace and quiet which they found with Him. And after He was gone they perceived that their religion consisted in a relationship to Him of a far more vital and wonderful kind than they had understood while He was here. For now they realized that it did not consist only in the mere memory of a good man who was gone, in the effort to recall the things which He had said, and to comfort their hearts with recollections of joyful hours of His flesh. They realized that it consisted in a living relationship to Him, as still a living person with them, while their faith was not a recollection of what Jesus had taught, or the mere memory of a lovely human character, but a unique relationship to an abiding, supernatural Person who had died for them and was their God and Saviour.

This is the fundamental thing in Christianity. As Karl Heim has said, "The essence of Christianity does not lie in a philosophy or a system of doctrine, nor in an ethic, but in a Person." The name "Christian" is only a sign of that which is most radical and essential in its character. The main problem of Christianity is this of Jesus Christ: Who was He, and what are we to think of Him? We cannot do any thinking about Christianity at all that is direct or adequate without coming at once to think of the problem of the Person of Jesus Christ, who stands at the heart of His religion, without whom the Christian religion is not the religion of Christ. Nay, far more than this is to be said. Christ is Christianity. Christianity is Christ. In the truest sense it is not a religion at all. Religion is the quest of man for God. Christianity is the quest of God for man. John Macmurray quotes a saying of Collingwood's *Speculum Mentis* to the effect that religion reached its climax in Christ and in doing so it ceased to be religion. When Christianity becomes a religion it ceases to be Christianity. It is not a human speculation about God. It is a divine revelation to man. It is either this or a gigantic misrepresentation on the part of Christianity and of Christ Himself. The whole issue is the issue of Christ. If He is true, Christianity is true. If He is not true, Christianity is not true. This is the fundamental question for each of us: "What is Christ's meaning to me?" We must ask and answer this question. Jesus Himself said so, "Whom do ye say that I am?"

There are many voices which tell us that this question is not primary and obligatory. I was in a gathering some time ago made up largely of college presidents and professors, in which the subject under discussion was the evangelical basis of the Young Men's Christian Association in our colleges and universities. It was a little company of fifteen or twenty men. One of the college presidents in the group, a minister in an evangelical church, expressed it as his own opinion that the question of the divinity of Jesus Christ was a matter of metaphysics about which we need not trouble ourselves and about which we had no right to burden the minds and consciences of the young men and women in our colleges and universities. We certainly had no right, he felt, to make a dividing intellectual issue of it.

Now if it is meant that the question of the deity of Christ is a matter of metaphysics in the sense that it lies beyond merely physical and material things, it is indeed a matter of metaphysics. But everything, for that matter, of any significance is metaphysical: friendship and love and truth and beauty and goodness are all metaphysical also. Everything that is worth while, everything that is real, all the unseen things that are the eternal things, are also metaphysical. If that was what the speaker meant, of course he was right. Christ's divinity also is metaphysical. But then, also, if that was what he meant he was wrong. Because these are the only things that it is most worth our while to think about at all. Indeed, we cannot do any thinking which is not metaphysical in that sense. But if he meant that the deity of Christ was metaphysical in the sense that it was impractical, that the conception carries us out into speculative regions where life is not lived, then he was utterly and absolutely wrong; for nothing can be more real, more practical, more near, more fundamental for every one of us than the question of what we are to think and what we are to do with the Person of Jesus Christ, who declared Himself to be, and is believed by the Church to be, the very Son of the living God.

We simply must think about that problem. We must think about it, for one thing, because Christ can have no meaning for feeling unless He has a meaning also for thought. As mature beings we cannot attach a feeling value to anything to which we cannot attach a thought value. "More Love to Thee, O Christ," has no meaning whatever except the meaning derived from the thought value we attach to Jesus Christ. If we think of Christ merely as we would think of Julius Cæsar, then the song has no more significance than if we were singing "More love to thee, O Julius Cæsar." All the meaning springs from the value we put upon Jesus Christ. Those men and women who tell us today that we can keep Christ for religious values even when we have lost Christ in His thought value are preaching a fallacious gospel, for Christ will stay with us in our religious life, He will stay with us as an adequate living value in our hearts, only so long as we give Him His rightful place in our thoughts about Him and His Person.

In the second place, we have to think about Christ and who He was because we are thinking beings, and wherever we go we have to take our minds along with us. I cannot go any place and leave my mind behind me. I cannot carry my body or my emotions into a certain attitude toward Christ without also carrying my rational processes along with me. I cannot take myself apart. I am a unit. I can only feel about those things that I think about and will about. It is impossible for me to have any relationship to Jesus Christ whatever except as I think about Christ and arrange my mind with reference to Him. It is intellectually maudlin and foolish to say "Christ" and "Christian" and "Christianity" unless we mean something by those words. What do we mean?

In the third place, we have got to think about Christ because He is a fact. We cannot get rid of a fact by saying, "I will not think about it." We look back across the years, and there stands Jesus demanding that we reckon with Him, that we give Him His place, that we think about Him, and relate Him to all the other facts that we know. Jesus Christ is not a doctrine; Jesus Christ is not a theory or a myth; Jesus Christ is not a mere imagination of men of our day; Jesus Christ is a great fact in history and in the life of men; and we are bound to think about that fact, to account for it and value it, to determine what the quality of that fact is, what the relations of that fact are to our present life today, and to all the life of humanity.

In the fourth place, Christ is not a mere fact of history. He is a moral issue that has to be faced. As Carnegie Simpson said in perhaps his most convincing book:

"What we find is this. We find that this fact of Christ, at all candidly considered in the conscience and the will, raises great moral issues within us. It is not merely that something in the example of Jesus or in His teaching has suggested a duty or made evident a defect. It is far more than that. It is that the problem of our whole moral life and character has been raised. The fact of Christ is not just a fact of history; it has become also a fact of conscience. It has arrested and arraigned our moral being; it has interrogated it; it has asserted itself as an authoritative reviewer of our life in the very fastnesses of our thoughts, our affections and our will. It does so with a strange inevitableness and with a remarkable right to do it. The more we candidly keep our minds and hearts and consciences open to the impression that even an historical appreciation of the fact of Christ makes upon them, the more does that impression turn to moral issues within us. We had thought intellectually to examine Him; we find He is spiritually examining us. The *rôles* are reversed between us. Not that historical and intellectual questions on our part about Jesus end, but far more serious and pressing and immediate are these moral questions about ourselves that have arisen out of them. All this is found true by many and many a one who simply reads the Gospels. It is a very singular phenomenon. We study Aristotle and are intellectually edified thereby; we study Jesus and are, in the profoundest way, spiritually disturbed. The question—apparently so innocently historical and morally non-committal—of 'What think ye of Christ?' passes into the most morally practical and personal of questions; 'What shall I then do with Him?' And this presses for an answer. . . . I think there is just ground for complaint when, for example, Keim describes Jesus as 'superhuman miracle' or Channing says he 'believes Jesus Christ to be more than a human being,' and there they leave the matter. One complains of this not in the orthodox but in a purely intellectual interest. These are meant to be serious and exact expressions, or they are not. If they are not seriously and exactly meant, they are intellectually unworthy evasions of the great problem of Christ. If they are serious and exact, they involve—let this be clearly understood—a position for which history has not the smallest support and philosophy has only utter repudiation."[1]

And once more, we have to think about this question because it was the question that interested Jesus Christ. So many times we are told today that it does not matter what men think, that it only matters what men do. It is a wonderful contrast to turn back to the Gospels and find Jesus reversing this emphasis. What men thought was what interested Him. He had no interest in a man's clothes; He had a secondary interest in a man's external acts. What did interest Him was what men had inside their hearts, because from within flowed the forces that were to determine the outer life. And so His great question, as He went up and down the world mingling with men, was the simple question, "What do you think about Me? Who am I?"

So, if we have never done any clear, consecutive thinking about Jesus Christ, we ought to begin to do that thinking now. There will come a time in our lives when we will have to do it. We must reckon with Jesus Christ and determine for ourselves whose Son we believe Him to be, and what conviction regarding His person we are to hold. Well would it be for us if today we should go straight home to what is not only the fundamental problem of Christianity but the very bottom-most issue of our human life, and face for ourselves that old question: Who is Jesus Christ? What do we believe Him to be? Was He in any unique sense the one Son of the Living God? And I want to state now in the simplest way I can, the grounds for my own personal faith in the deity of our Lord Jesus Christ.

---

[1] P. Carnegie Simpson, *The Fact of Christ,* pp. 34, 35, 86 (Revell).

I. I believe, first of all, in the deity of Christ because of His character; for it seems to me, in the great language of Horace Bushnell, that "the character of Jesus forbids His possible classification with men." The argument of the whole volume, *Nature and the Supernatural,* is concentrated by Bushnell in that one chapter, "The Character of Jesus Forbidding His Possible Classification with Men," already mentioned. It is worth while to record Bushnell's own outline of the argument of this wonderful chapter:

"The superhuman personality of Christ is fully attested by His character. And the description verifies itself. Represented as beginning with a perfect childhood, which childhood is described naturally and without exaggeration of fancy. Represented always as an innocent being, yet without loss of force. His purity is unrepentant and yet successfully maintained. He united characters which men are never able to unite perfectly. His amazing pretensions are sustained so as never even to shock the sceptic. Excels as truly in the passive virtues. Bears the common trials in a faultless manner of patience. His passion, as regards the time and the intensity, is not human. His undertaking to organize on earth a Kingdom of God is superhuman. His plan is universal in time. He takes rank with the poor and begins with them for His material. Becoming the head, then, of a class, He never awakens a partisan feeling. His teachings are perfectly original and independent. He teaches by no human or philosophic methods. He never runs to catch the assent of multitudes. He is comprehensive in the widest sense. He is perfectly clear of superstition in a superstitious age. He is no liberal, yet shows a perfect charity. The simplicity of His teaching is perfect. His morality is not artificial or artistic. He is never anxious for His success. He impresses His superiority and His real greatness the more deeply, the more familiarly He is known. Did any such character exist or is it a myth of human invention? Is the character sinless? Mr. Parker and Mr.

Hennel think Him imperfect. Answer of Milton to one of their accusations. How great a matter that one such character has lived in the world."

Philip Schaff, in his study of *The Person of Christ,* has gone beyond the matter of the human character and dealt with issues to which we will a little later come, but the outline of his argument falls here beside Bushnell's:

"Christ's name is in fact above every other name. He was perfect in the midst of an imperfect world. He comes before us as a child, a combination of humility and grandeur, yet no unnatural prodigy. He was acquainted with no literature except the Old Testament and confined Himself strictly to religion, yet sheds light over the whole world of man and nature. He speaks from divine intuition and is the truth. He has an authority that commands attention. He did all in the fresh vigour of early manhood. His Gospel never wearies nor is exhausted. His ministry has boundless historic meaning. He moved in the circle of every-day life and selected His disciples from the lowly. He produced incalculable effects and now controls the destiny of the civilized world. He is an unsolvable problem unless He is the Son of God. He was tempted, but never yielded. His relative sinlessness became absolute sinlessness. He attained a moral impossibility of sinning. He shows no wrong or sin. He is positively just and holy. He was consciously sinless. He differed from all others not in degree only, but in kind. The sublime moral miracle of history. He was seen in all situations and sustained the same consistent character throughout. He finished the work given Him to do. Under His influence His disciples became great benefactors and teachers. He idealized the child spirit. In His relation with women He combined purity with familiarity and tenderness. He represented unbroken unity and communion with God. He was a man not of inactive contemplation but of practical activity. He arose above all prejudices and bigotries. He was free from one-sidedness, not a man of one idea, nor of any one temperament. His virtue was healthy, manly, vigorous, yet genial, social, winning. His qualities were in perfect balance; zeal never degenerating into passion, childish innocence combined with manly strength, fearless courage with wise caution. He was the most radical and yet the most conservative of reformers. He was complete in suffering. He exalted forgiveness and submission. He bore pain and death superhumanly, in a divine glory of spirit, with a commanding grandeur and majesty. The supernatural in Him was an inherent power. He founded a spiritual kingdom. He sets forth His amazing claims as self-evident truths. He Himself shines with self-evidencing light."

Christ was such a Man that He could not have been a mere man. He was a Man so great, so perfect, that He must have been more than just a man. Now we can put the matter in a very summary fashion at this point. If our Lord was only a man, if His character was merely human, then Bowdoin, Yale, Bryn Mawr, and Vassar ought to be turning out better men and women than He was. If our Lord was only a man, it is strange that the nineteenth century cannot produce a better one. He was born in an obscure and despised province. He grew up in no cultured and refined community. He was the child of a poor peasant's home, of a subject race. Yet He rises sheer above all mankind, the one commanding moral character of humanity. Now, if Jesus was all that, just as a mere man, the world should long ago have advanced beyond Him.

It would not be so if it were a question of intellectual genius, because we all realize that intellectual genius is a matter of endowment and gift, and a man cannot be held responsible for not being as able a man intellectually as another. But we all feel that each of us can be held responsible for not being as good a man as any other man. We know that moral character is a duty of each one of us, and there is nothing in moral goodness which our own conscience does not tell us we are bound ourselves to attain. With nineteen hundred years of His influence upon the world, with advantages possessed by us such as were never dreamed of in His day, if Christ's character was purely human, it ought long ago to have been surpassed and there ought to be in the world today many men and women who are superior in character to Him.

This is a crude, though proper dilemma. If Christ was only a man we are bound to surpass Him. If He was more than a man, we are bound to obey Him. We cannot let the point go merely with this general statement, however. I believe that Jesus Christ is the Son of God, proved to be such by the elements of character in Him not to be found in men.

(1) First of all, there was the supernaturalness of His claims. "I am come that ye might have life." "I am the light of the world." "I am not come to condemn, but to save the world." "I am the way, and the truth, and the life: no man cometh unto the Father but by Me." Now a man cannot talk that way. If you should say in reply that the words quoted are from the Gospel of John, and that they do not actually represent what Jesus said but only what John afterwards put into His lips, we should demur; but without stopping to do so, we would say now, Very well, turn to the Gospel of Matthew and find the passage which criticism still leaves to us, in which Christ says just as much as He says anywhere in the Gospel of John: "All things have been delivered unto Me of My Father: and no one knoweth the Son, save the Father; neither doth any know the Father save the Son, and he to

whomsoever the Son willeth to reveal Him. Come unto Me, all ye that labour and are heavy laden, and I will give you rest. Take My yoke upon you, and learn of Me; for I am meek and lowly in heart: and ye shall find rest unto your souls." There is supernatural claim here just such as in the deepest of our Lord's utterances in the Gospel of John. Or, turn to the Sermon on the Mount. It is full of unique self-assertion. Who is this young man who stands on the shores of the Galilean Sea and sets aside the doctrines of the fathers? "Ye have heard it said so and so, but I say unto you;" and who closes His discourse with the declaration, "Many will say unto Me in that day, Lord, Lord, did we not cast out devils in Thy name? and I will say unto them, I never knew you, depart from Me"? Who is this who thus sets Himself up as the very touchstone of eternal destiny in the day of judgment?

Our Lord by His claims set Himself in a class absolutely apart from men.[2] Now He either made these

---

[2] *Cf.* Hoskyns and Davey, *The Riddle of the New Testament* (Harcourt and Brace).

"We must therefore conclude that Jesus Himself did not think of His Life and Death as a human achievement at all. Language descriptive of human heroism is entirely foreign to the New Testament. The Event of the Life and Death of Jesus was not thought of as a human act, but as an act of God wrought out in human flesh and blood, which is a very different matter. The Event was conceived of as a descending act of God, not as the ascending career of a man who was successful in the sphere of religion. No New Testament writer could think of Jesus in Pelagian terms. The concrete Event, which was Jesus of Nazareth, was for them the sphere in which God had effected a mighty action for the salvation of men. Again, this was no mere piece of theologizing, but the very way in which Jesus Himself regarded His ministry. Human flesh and blood, words and actions, were, as it were, caught up, controlled, energized by the Spirit of God, by the Son of God, so that St. Paul could speak of Christ Jesus as Him in whom 'dwelleth all the fulness of the Godhead bodily,' just as the author of the Fourth Gospel could write of the Word claims or He did not make them. If He did not make them, then we know nothing whatever about His life, and what took place in the past, for the evidence of the fact that Christ made these claims is as good as any historical evidence that we possess. If He did make these claims, they were either true or false. If they were false, then Christ instead of being a man of high character, as all men have recognized Him to be, was a mere falsifier, an imposter. But if they were

---

becoming flesh. This emphatic assertion that Jesus is the sphere of the action of God presumes the Theocentric atmosphere in which Jesus lived and died. His obedience was surrender to the unique and active operation of the Living God. This was expressed by Him by the relation of the Father to the Beloved or Only-Begotten Son" (pp. 254, 255 f.).

"It must be quite definitely affirmed that neither the Jesus of History nor the Primitive Church fits into the characteristic nexus of modern popular humanitarian or humanistic ideas. This is not merely because they belong to another age, of which the thought moved in an entirely unmodern idiom, but because their idiom was entirely foreign to that of any age, including their own. The Gospel was as much a scandal to the first century as it is to the twentieth. This does not mean, however, that the Gospel is in any sense anti-humanitarian. The antithesis between it and modern idealism arises, not because Jesus and Primitive Christianity were less human than humanitarianism, but because they were infinitely more so. The Primitive Christians found the revelation of God in an historical figure so desperately human that there emerged within the early Church a faith in men and women so deeply rooted as to make modern humanitarianism seem doctrinaire and trivial. The New Testament does not present a complex chaos of conceptions about God and man from which one or another may be picked out and proclaimed as ultimate and true because it satisfies the highest idealism of this or of all ages; it presents a concrete and definite solution of the problems of Life and Death, of Right and Wrong, of Happiness and Misery, in a form which constitutes a challenge to all thought and to all ethical idealism. The New Testament presents the solution in a unique Event, in a particular history of human flesh and blood. The New Testament is therefore neither a collection of thoughtful essays nor an attempt to construct a system of ethics. It bears witness to a unique History, and it discovers the Truth in the History. The historian is compelled to state the unity and uniqueness of this staggering claim as an historical fact" (p. 261 f.).

true, then He was, as He claimed to be, the Son of God.

(2) Observe further, not only did Jesus put forth supernatural claims, but those claims were attested by His own consciousness. Let any of us set ourselves up to be divine and see how quickly we will fall to the earth from any such pinnacle. Our own deeds would belie us and our own consciousness break down under the palpable falsehood. In Acre, Syria, the head of the Behais, Abbas Effendi, actually claimed to be God the Father incarnate on earth. But he simply could not carry it through. He could not bear himself god-likely. But we look on the outer and even more on the inner life of Christ. It actually sustained the tremendous, world-upheaving claims that He put forth to be the unique, supernatural Son of the living God. Men are turning now as never before to the study of Christ's consciousness, the most wonderful prbolem in human history, and they are finding in the inner thought of Christ and the inner life of Christ, in the integrity of it, in the way in which He was able to carry through to the end His tremendous claims, a new argument for the truth and reality of these claims. How clearly it shone out at the last when hanging upon the cross, with the two thieves on either side of Him, He died like the God He had claimed to be, so that the hard-hearted centurion, who stood and watched Him die, exclaimed, "Well, I have seen many a man die, but I never saw one who died like this. Truly this man was the Son of God." But the manner of His death only consummated the sustained sincerity of His life. I believe in the deity of Christ on the score of His character not only because He put forth claims to be supernaturally unique, but be-

cause His own inner spiritual experience supported and vindicated these claims.

(3) And because of the universality of His character, I believe in the deity of Jesus Christ. Of course He had to be born in a given age, among a given people, and He was born in the first century and in the Jewish race. It was impossible that there should be an incarnation without its being somewhere and somewhen. But the wonderful thing is, that though Christ came in a given age and in a given race He transcends that age and that race and is felt by every age and every race to be its ideal and its Lord, the satisfaction of all its spiritual needs. We see this aspect of His character illustrated in the universality and eternity of the sympathies that find expression in His parables. A book of illustrations of the parables appeared some years ago. They were by a modern artist. He had taken eight or ten of the parables out of their ancient Oriental setting and given them a modern Western setting. One of them was a picture of a girl sitting in a restaurant with wine glasses on the table before her. Another girl, a Salvation Army lass, was coming through with her tambourine, collecting gifts. Beneath were the words: "Five of them were wise, and five of them were foolish." Another was the picture of the Pharisee and the publican. The poor man was sitting in ragged clothes in the last pew of the church, and the wealthy man, standing in his self-contentment and power, was taking the collection and holding the plate at a distance for this poor man to put his coin in. Another was the picture of the man with the talents. A young man sat alone at his club, with bowed head, while round about him the air was filled with figures of others who had toiled, while the opportunities of

his life had been lost and thrown away; and beneath was the simple verse taken from our Lord's parable of the talents: "And he went and hid his talent in a napkin and buried it in the ground." These parables come driving right home into the heart of our modern life as though they had been spoken today. And these parables of our Lord's, spoken nineteen hundred years ago, cast first of all in His native setting in the East, but always and everywhere alive, are only typical of the universality and eternity of His loving sympathies. He is the world's still unattained ethical ideal. He is still the friend of all. The first century Jew is the whole world's and all the centuries' Saviour.

(4) And from the perfect balance of His character I believe that Jesus Christ is the Divine Son of God. Everyone has some of the characteristics of Christ, but no one has all of them. We develop one good quality at the expense or the atrophy or the stricture of some other quality. Our Lord bound up in Himself all the different qualities of the perfect human character as no other has ever done. As Bushnell wrote:

"The more closely He is drawn to other worlds, the more fresh and susceptible is He to the humanities of this. The little child is an image of gladness which His heart leaps forth to embrace. The wedding, the feast, and the funeral have each their cords of sympathy in His bosom. At the wedding He is clothed in congratulations, at the feast in doctrine, at the funeral in tears; but no miser was ever drawn to his money with stronger desire than He to worlds above. Men undertake to be spiritual and they become ascetic; or, endeavouring to hold a liberal view of the comforts and pleasures of society, they are soon buried in the world and slaves to its fashions; or, holding a scrupulous watch to keep out every particular sin, they become legal and fall out of liberty; or, charmed with the noble and heavenly liberty, they run to negligence and irresponsible living: so the earnest become violent, the fervent fanatical, the gentle waver, the firm turn bigots, the liberal grow lax, the benevolent ostentatious. Poor human infirmity can hold nothing steady. Where the pivot of righteousness is broken, the scales must needs slide off their balance. Indeed, it is one of the most difficult things which a cultivated Christian can attempt, only to sketch a theoretic view of character in its true justness and proportion, so that a little more study or a little more self-experience will not require him to modify it; and yet the character of Christ is never modified even by a shade of rectification. It is one and the same throughout. He makes no improvements, prunes no extravagances, returns from no eccentricities. The balance of His character is never disturbed or readjusted, and the astounding assumption on which it is based is never shaken even by a suspicion that He falters in it." [3]

(5) But not to prolong an analysis of His character unduly, think of only one other outstanding fact in it, the fact of His sinlessness. No other great teacher ever dared to utter Jesus' challenge: "Which of you convinceth Me of sin." No one has thought of claiming sinlessness for other great religious teachers. In none of the sacred books of any other religion is its founder represented as a sinless man. The very conception of a sinless character was never invented by anybody. It only came to men's minds as they saw it worked forth in the character of Jesus of Nazareth. There is marvellous significance in this fact. He was the holiest man that ever lived. Everybody looks back upon Him as the most wonderfully perfect character. And He was the one Man who was never penitent, who never asked God to forgive Him for anything, who walked right through life unrepentant, without

[3] Bushnell, *The Character of Jesus*, pp. 21, 22 (Scribners).

ever being aware that He had done or thought anything wrong. "Father, forgive them," He prayed, but never "Father, forgive Me." Find a single great human character whose goodness does not rest on a sense of utter personal unworthiness, whose goodness does not spring from the deep realization of having been forgiven much by the great and loving God. But here is Jesus of Nazareth, the one character to whom we all look back as the best of men, absolutely impenitent, and He died impenitent because there was nothing in His life for which He needed to ask forgiveness. If any one can believe that this character was merely human, then he is a very credulous soul. To believe that this character was merely human is a belief more wonderful, involving more strain to human faith, than the simple conviction that we can account for the character of Christ by believing Him to be what He claimed to me; namely, the Son of the Living God.

II. In the second place, I believe in the deity of Christ because of His teaching; not only because of the form and authority of His teaching—though that was wonderful enough to impress in the deepest way the imagination of those who heard Him—for He taught, as Matthew recorded in comment on the Sermon on the Mount," as one having authority and not as the Scribes." "This man spake," said those sent by the Sanhedrin to arrest Him, "as never man spake." But I am thinking now not of the form and the power of His teaching, but of the substance of it. I believe the substance of Christ's teaching sets Him apart from the class of mere human teachers.

(1) First of all, consider His teaching regarding God. Where did He find out what He knew about God? He taught things about God which the world

never knew before, and which the world had not been able to discover for itself. Today, as a matter of fact, almost the whole content of our knowledge of God is due to the teaching, the life, and the example of Jesus Christ. There is something to be learned about God from the heavens and the world round about us. But in the case of people who deny the divinity of Christ and who say they believe in God, that God in whom they believe is the God about whom they would know little or nothing if Jesus Christ had not come and revealed Him by what He was, as well as by what He said. You cannot reveal God by words; you cannot bring to men an idea entirely outside their experience simply by talking to them in words; you have to show it to them in life. Christ could never have revealed God by a mere doctrine. He could not by any possibility have broken open the shell of man's limited notions of God and expanded these notions to the great realities to which He did expand them, by merely proclaiming intellectual opinions concerning God. You can give men a new idea of God only by showing it to them in life. "The Word was made flesh and dwelt among us and we beheld His glory." There is no other way. It is the way in which Christ "declared" God nineteen hundred years ago—not by talking about the idea, but by Himself being this God in front of their eyes. "He that hath seen Me hath seen the Father." [4] (*Cf.* John i:18.)

And here we come upon what is the sad irony of human history; that Jesus Christ Himself has created the difficulty in the way of men's faith in His deity. We ask men why they do not believe in the incarna-

---

[4] See testimony of Richard Holt Hutton in appendix to this chapter.

tion today, and they tell us that they cannot believe that their God, so spiritual, so high, could be brought down into humanity. Where did they get that God so spiritual and so high? Why, only out of the God who was incarnate in humanity. The mere fact of this larger idea of God which Christ by the Incarnation gave is now made by many men the reason why they will not believe in Christ and the Incarnation, through which, in fact, that idea of God historically came to us. We would not have such difficulty in believing in Christ as God, if Christ had not been God. It was the very fact that Christ was God that gave us these notions of God that have created, not wholly, but in large part, the difficulties in the way of our faith in the Incarnation. Surely the man who will sit down and contemplate the revelation of God in Christ and think all the implications of the situation through must at last say to himself exactly what Thomas said when his eyes at last were opened, "My Lord and my God."

(2) And I believe in the deity of Christ not only because of His teaching about God, but also because of His teaching about man. He told us things about man that we never knew before, that are not known in the world today except where the influence of Christ's life has reached, bringing them to man. It was only Christ who told man what a good man may be and must be, who gave man his ideal of his own duty and destiny and possibility of character. It was only Christ who came near to man and assured him of that spiritual possibility and duty of unity with his fellows, that has become one of the great words of our time, but of which in reality we have come to conceive only through the influence of Jesus Christ. A

German ethnologist once said that the deepest thing ever uttered by Saint Paul is that word of his about there being in Jesus Christ "neither male nor female, Greek nor barbarian, bond nor free." These were the three great lines of cleavage that cursed the world before Christ, that curse the world everywhere now outside of Christ, and that were obliterated by Christ's new revelation to man of his relation to his brother.

(3) I believe also in the deity of Christ not only on the ground of His teaching about God and man but also because of His ethical teaching. We have conceded far too much in the study of comparative ethics to the non-Christian religions. Not only are the non-Christian religions destitute of our Lord's great teaching about God and man, but they do not have in them those fundamental moral and social and spiritual principles which Christ brought, and over which He poured a flood of illuminating glory from God. Take Christ's great ethical conceptions, such as truth and duty and purity and love and righteousness, and where can you find in any of the non-Christian religions conceptions in any wise equalling them? We can rest our argument for the deity of Christ, for His absolute separateness from man, on the ground of the magnitude and uniqueness of His contribution to the moral life alone. On God and man and morals He has spoken the last word. "The attempt to add to or improve on the teaching of Christ," Lord Avebury recognizes, "seems vain and even arrogant." On the ground, accordingly, not only of what He was, but also of what He taught, I believe in the deity of our Lord Jesus Christ.

III. In the third place, not alone on the ground of His character and doctrine, but on the ground of the acts which He did while here on earth, I believe in the deity of Christ. I am not speaking now of His miracles on nature, though I have no trouble with them; they are exactly the things which I believe God incarnate in human flesh would do. But I pass them by to speak about what He did on human life. There is the miracle of His influence on the twelve apostles. He took those men—barring, of course, the one who failed Him—ignorant, unlettered, with no early advantages, fishermen many of them, adult men when He took them under His influence, and made these hard men the finest and most creative spirits of their time. He sent out this uneducated, uninfluential group to shake and shape the world. He made them the foundations on which He built His indestructible kingdom. Where can we find a greater miracle than that? He made other men and women also, and His work on life was crowned at the last by the outstanding miracle of His own Resurrection. I believe there is no fact in ancient history better attested than our Lord's Resurrection. I believe that we may rest as securely on the evidences of the Resurrection as we may on the evidence that there was ever a Declaration of Independence. You say, we have it now. We have a living Christ now. You say, men saw it signed. Men saw Him risen. You say, there is a nation living whose existence testifies to the Declaration of Independence. There is a kingdom of Christ in existence that bears witness to the fact that something lifted it out of the death in which it lay when He hung upon His cross. It was saved by nothing less than His rising again from the dead. Without a risen Christ there is no adequate explanation of the resurrection of Christianity. You say the historic evidence does not satisfy everyone. It convinces all who would be convinced if they saw

Him rise with their own eyes. Because of what He did while here upon the earth, I believe Him to be the Son of God.

IV. Further, I believe in the deity of Christ because of His posthumous influence. He is doing in the world still things just as wonderful as anything He did in the world nineteen hundred years ago. Napoleon turned once at St. Helena to Count Montholon with the inquiry, "Can you tell me who Jesus Christ was?" The question was declined, and Napoleon proceeded, "Well, then, I will tell you. Alexander, Cæsar, Charlemagne, and I have founded great empires, but upon what did these creations of our genius depend? Upon force! Jesus alone founded His empire upon love, and to this very day millions would die for Him. . . . I think I understand something of human nature, and I tell you all these were men and I am a man. None else is like Him. Jesus Christ was more than a man. . . . I have inspired multitudes with such a devotion that they would have died for me . . . but to do this it was necessary that I should be visibly present, with the electric influence of my looks, of my words, of my voice. When I saw men and spoke to them I lighted up the flames of self-devotion in their hearts. . . . Christ alone has succeeded in so raising the mind of man towards the unseen that it becomes insensible to the barriers of time and space. Across a chasm of eighteen hundred years Jesus Christ makes a demand which is, above all others, difficult to satisfy. He asks for that which a philosopher may often seek in vain at the hands of his friends, or a father of his children, or a bride of her spouse, or a man of his brother. He asks for the human heart. He will have it entirely to Himself. He demands it unconditionally, and forthwith His demand is granted. Wonderful! In defiance of time and space, the soul of man with all its powers becomes an annexation to the empire of Christ. All who sincerely believe in Him experience that remarkable supernatural love towards Him. This phenomenon is unaccountable; it is altogether beyond the scope of man's creative powers. Time, the great destroyer, is powerless to extinguish the sacred flame; time can neither exhaust its strength nor put a limit to its range. This it is which strikes me most. I have often thought of it. This it is which proves to me quite conclusively the divinity of Jesus Christ."

We see today in the world a work being done that no man could do. Julius Cæsar is not raising dead men today. Martin Luther is not taking men dead in trespasses and sins and washing them white as the very snows, redeeming them to new and powerful life. Christ is doing that today. He is taking the roué and the debauchee out of the gutter, and He is making them pure and sending them out with cleansed consciences to do the work of men in the world. He is taking the weakling, the man or woman with no strength of character, without enough strength of passion to go down into the gutter, and He moulds them to strength and usefulness. And He is redeeming good people, which is the most wonderful thing of all. He is taking the proud and the selfish and the pitiless, He is taking the rich who have everything and do not know that they are poor, the clothed who think they are clothed and do not know that they are naked—Christ is taking them and revealing the realities of their own life to them and giving them the realities of His life. And what no man ever did—Christ is releasing men from the shame and guilt of sin as well as delivering them from its power. This work which we see Christ doing today in the lives of men is no human work. Today, as of old, Christ is transforming character and nature, doing the work of God on the life of man.

Christ is still, as He has always been, the great transformer of the life of the world. We cannot explain the influence with which Christ has wrought upon the life of the world on the theory of His merely human character. Buddhism, Hinduism, Confucianism, Mohammedanism by their results have proved that their founders, whatever they may have been as men, were not divine. But Christ has been doing here a work which only God could do. He has changed the world. So far as it has changed for good, it is Christ who has changed it. He has reconstructed human society. He has created and sustained the highest moral life. His living principles have ordered all true human progress. It is far more irrational to attribute these effects to inadequate causes than it is to say that they must have a cause adequate to produce them. They have not flowed from man's inherent and self-unfolding perfectibility. They are the work of God; by the hand of God they must have been done. Those who have experienced them in their own souls know that it was by God in Christ that they were done.

V. And now, last of all, why is it that if we have grounds for belief in the deity of Christ such as these there are so many men and women who do not believe that Christ is the Son of God? Well, in the first place, some of them have never done any thinking about it. They have listened to what other people have said, and what the other people have said was only what they heard somebody else say. They themselves have never done any real, conscientious, consecutive reflection on the problem of Christ at all. Some of our want of faith in Christ simply springs from shallowness, superficiality, or intellectual neglect.

In the second place, a great many have no adequate conception of the person of Christ simply because they have never studied the original documents. If you will saturate your mind and heart with the four Gospels for twelve months, if you will read them through, all four every week, and not only read them but dwell upon the character of Christ as it comes out in them, letting your imagination play with the freedom of the Spirit of life upon that life of Christ, that word of Christ, that personality of Christ, you will come back twelve months from now with your faith in the deity of Christ as the Son of God established unassailably.

In the third place, a great many do not believe in His deity simply because they do not know how absolutely the world needs God incarnate in the flesh. I had a friend who said that he never realized how it must be that Christ was the Son of God until during his university course he went to work in the county jail. Sunday after Sunday as he sat down among the prisoners in the jail, among men of darkened souls, men of rotted-out characters, men who were hopeless about this world and the world to come, men who were as dead as any man could ever be when his body was laid in his grave, he realized as he had never realized before that, if there never had been an incarnation, by the very need of man and the character of God there must be one; because it was necessary that there should come into the world somewhere and sometime such a release of divine and transforming power as the world in its death could never live without. We believe it came nineteen hundred years ago adequately and once for all in Jesus of Nazareth.

And lastly, there are men and women who do not believe in the deity of Christ simply because they have never tried Him. The deity of Christ is not a mere doctrine or proposition. It is a living theory of being, and the way you test it is not alone to go back and examine these evidences which we have been running over in this hasty and inadequate way. The way you test it is to try Christ whether He is what He claims to be. In *The Sunday School Times* years ago Edward Everett Hale, Jr., wrote an article on the change wrought in him by his experience of Jesus Christ as the Son of God. He had not grown up to believe in the deity of Christ—far otherwise. But he had done his thinking for himself, and at last he came one night in a little prayer-meeting in the city of Schenectady, where he lived, to the point where he made up his mind that the only way to find out was to experiment. He put Christ to the test and he found Him divinely true and truly divine.[5] If what has been said here could only so far remove the intellectual difficulties which any one may feel as to make it possible for him to put Christ to the test, he too would find Him true.

No one leaned on Him in vain when He was here; no one leans on Him in vain today. Would that we might see Him in the fulness of His glory as He is: Son of Man, indeed, Son of God as well; Son of Man because only so could God ever come near us and lay hold of our lives and assure us that His will for us was what we see in Christ; Son of God because only so could we ever get strength to rise into God. "Who

---

[5] See appendix to this chapter.

say ye that I am?" was the question He asked Simon Peter by Cæsarea Philippi of old. "And who say ye that I am?" is the question He is asking of each of us here now. God grant that the same Father who revealed the truth to Simon Peter that day may enable us to behold the truth today, that we may answer as he answered, "Thou art the Christ, the Son of the living God." That is what He is. Is He that to us?

THREE SUPPLEMENTARY NOTES TO CHAPTER II

I. On Christ's Self-Assertion and Lowliness.
II. On the Inadequacy of the Unitarian View.
III. Professor Edward Everett Hale's Experience.

ON CHRIST'S SELF-ASSERTION AND LOWLINESS

The late Richard Holt Hutton, editor of *The Spectator*, in his essay on "Christian Evidences," speaks of the supernaturalness of Christ's foresight in perceiving that these extraordinary claims of His would be accepted by men and be found by them to be entirely consistent with His lowliness of soul. "That Christ should have understood the personal relation in which His immediate disciples would stand to Him," says Mr. Hutton, "was perhaps a mere instance of discernment such as, no doubt, many great men have shown. But that He should deliberately have demanded the same kind of attitude towards Himself from all future disciples, as He certainly did, and have gained what He asked in the very act, does seem to me one of the clearest marks of supernatural knowledge of the human heart which could be given. Nothing could be more hazardous than this emphasis laid by any human being—especially one who from the very first preaches lowliness of heart, and predicts the shortness of His life and the ignominious violence of His end—on Himself as the source of an enduring power, and the corner-stone of a divine kingdom. The necessity of loving Him, the perpetual fame of her who anointed Him for His burial, the grief that will be rightly felt for Him when He leaves the earth, the identification of men's duty to each other, even to 'the least of these, My brethren,' with their duty to Him—all these are assumptions which run through the whole Gospel quite as strikingly as does the clear knowledge of the frailty of the human materials Christ has chosen, and of the supernatural character of the power by which He intended to vivify those means. Though His kingdom is to be the kingdom of which a little child is the type, the kingdom in which it is the 'meek' who are blessed, in which it is the 'poor in spirit' who are to be the rulers, yet in this He is only saying in other words, that He is to be the life of it, since it is because He is 'meek and lowly in heart' that those who come to Him shall find rest to their souls. Whether you choose to say that it is in spite of this humility or because of this humility, yet in either case Christ proclaims Himself as the true object of love, and the permanent centre of power throughout the kingdom He proclaims. He not only declares that His departure will be the first legitimate cause of mourning to His followers—'Can the children of the bride-chamber mourn as long as the bridegroom is with them? But the days will come when the bridegroom shall be taken from them, and then shall they fast'—but even to all others the love of Him is to predominate over all other love. 'He that loveth father or mother more than Me is not worthy of Me, and he that loveth son or daughter more than Me is not worthy of Me.' Exclusion from His presence is everywhere treated as that outer darkness where there are weeping and gnashing of teeth. His vision of the spiritual future of untrue men is of men crying to Him, 'Lord, Lord!' and entreating Him to recognize them, to whom He will be compelled to say, 'I never knew you; depart from Me, ye that work iniquity.' He justifies with warmth all honour paid to him personally; 'The poor ye have always with you, but Me ye have not always;' 'Verily, I say wherever this gospel shall be preached in the whole world, there shall also this, which this woman hath done, be told for a memorial of her.' Is not that most hazardous policy for any one not endowed with supernatural knowledge? Consider only what usually comes with self-assertion much less astounding than this in a human being, and yet what actually came of it in our Lord's case. The greatest of the world's teachers made light of themselves. Socrates treats his own death as of no moment. The Jewish prophets never think of treating their own careers as of any significance apart from the message they deliver. And as a rule in the world, when a man magnifies himself with gentleness and simplicity, we smile; we may find him lovable, but there is always a little laughter mingled with our love. When he does it arrogantly or imperiously, we are revolted. In either case, the first generation which does not personally know him puts aside his pretensions as irrelevant, if not even fatal, to his greatness. But how was it with Christ? The first great follower who had never known Him in the flesh, St. Paul, takes up this very note as the key-note of the new world. To him 'to live is Christ, to die is gain.' His heart is 'hid with Christ in God.' His cry is, 'Not I, but Christ that worketh in me.' He makes his whole religious philosophy turn on the teaching of our Lord, that He is the Vine, and His disciples the branches. In the land of the olive St. Paul adapts the image to the husbandry of the olive. Again, Christ is the Head, and men the members. And what is true of S. Paul is true of all those in whom the Christian faith has shown its highest genius in subsequent ages. These sayings of Christ as to Himself the centre of human affections and the light of human lives, instead of repelling men, interpret their own highest experience, and seem but the voice of an interior truth and the assurance of an imperishable joy."

ON THE INADEQUACY OF THE UNITARIAN VIEW

There are deeper considerations than these of which I have spoken for rejecting the Unitarian view of the person of Jesus Christ. Mr. Hutton sets these forth as the reason for Maurice's departure from the Unitarianism of his father. "What then," asks he in an essay on *Maurice and the Unitarians,* "is meant by saying that Maurice's rejection of Unitarianism was the result of an ardent yearning after a centre of more perfect unity with others,—others generally differing from himself,—than he had ever been able to find in Unitarianism? It meant just this, that Maurice regarded the self-revelation of God, within whose eternal nature there is something more complex and more mysterious than merely lonely will and lonely power, as the best guarantee of which he could conceive for the mutual affections and the mutual forbearances of human society; and that he believed that such a gradual revelation was actually made to man in the Providential story of Jewish history as it culminated in the life and death and resurrection of Christ. . . . The reason he was dissatisfied with Unitarianism was simply this,—that Unitarianism, even as his father understood it, explained away a great part of the actual revelation made by God to man, and therefore attenuated its importance and the trust and hope with which it inspired him. It was not that he thought himself any holier than Unitarians. On the contrary, he thought many Unitarians holier than himself. But he held that the history contained in the Bible pointed to something much more mysterious and much more adequate to the need, and guilt, and passion of human nature, in the character of the divine life which it revealed, than anything which the Unitarians could find in that history, and therefore he held the Unitarian interpretation of that history to be a pallid one, which missed a good part of its true burden, and especially that part of it which is most essential to promote the true unity of men, and to add depth and intensity to the social relations. He admits in a letter to his father that Unitarianism is a much *simpler* account of the revelation given in the Bible than his own faith. But then, what it gains in simplicity it loses in adequacy, both as regards the actual language of Scripture, and also as regards that actual life in man in its appeal to which the language of Scripture is so potent. 'It is simpler,' he says, 'to believe in a Great Spirit with the North American Indians, it is simpler to worship wood and stone; but what is the worth of simplicity, if it does not satisfy wants which we feel, if it does not lead us up to the truth which we desire?' The prophecies of the many predecessors of Christ were to Maurice unintelligible, if they represented nothing but the foreshadowings of a great 'exemplar,' and the life of Christ was still less intelligible as the mere life of that great exemplar. Either this long history, with its great catastrophe, meant something a great deal more expressive of that groaning and travailing of creation to which Paul referred, than the coming of an exemplar, or else a great deal less than the Unitarianism of the elder Maurice represented it to be. Maurice believed that it meant a great deal more, and not a great deal less, than his father and the Unitarians generally understood by it; that it meant the deliberate unfolding of the nature and life of God with such power and passion as to inspire in man a transforming trust and a united love. Maurice did not, of course, expect that any theological belief could be the centre of unity; but he did expect that, if God were what he held that Scripture declared God to be, God Himself would be that centre of unity, because it showed God to be spending on the reconciliation of men to Himself the infinite stores of that divine passion of which we find our only adequate type in Gethsemane and on Calvary." The Incarnation, as Mr. Hutton, who himself had passed over from the Unitarian view to an absolute acceptance of the deity of Christ, argues elsewhere, in *The Incarnation and Principles of Evidence*, is necessary to reveal to us, as I have already declared it did reveal to us, both the nature of God and the nature of man. We know neither God nor ourselves apart from the divine Christ. "I believe then," says Mr. Hutton, "that the revelation of God through an Eternal Son would realize to us, if it can be adequately believed, that the relation of God to us is only the manifestation of His life in itself, as it was or would be without us—'before all worlds,' as the theologians say; that 'before all worlds,' He was essentially the Father, essentially Love, essentially something infinitely more than Knowledge or Power, essentially communicating and receiving a living affection, essentially all that the heart can desire. This is not, then, relative truth for us only, but the truth as it is in itself, the reality of Infinite Being. It is first proclaimed to us, indeed, to save us from sin, strengthen us in frailty, and lift us above ourselves; but it could not do this as it does, did we not know that God was, and His love was, and His Fatherly Life was, apart from man, and that it is a reality infinitely deeper and vaster than the existence of His human children.

"And it seems to me that to know God to be in His own essential nature a Father, not merely a Father to us, is a very great step towards exalting the whole tone of our actual life. We are apt to take the word 'Father' as metaphorical in its application to God—a metaphor derived from human parentage. But such a faith teaches us that the most sacred human relations, which we feel to be far deeper than any individual and solitary human attributes, are but faint shadows of realities eternally existing in the divine mind. It is customary in many philosophical schools to regard the 'absoluteness' of God, the absence of all relation to Him, as a part of His divine *privilege*. To me such a conception appears essentially atheistic, if really thought out, though, of course, practically consistent with the most genuine and fervent piety. Judaism never did think it out without hovering on the very margin of the discovery which Christ made to us. That discovery was, as it seems to me, in one aspect of it—that aspect in which it could be made only through an Eternal Son of God—this: 'Never try to think of Me,' it seems to say, 'as a mere Sovereign Will; never try to conceive My Infinitude as exclusive of all divine life, except My own; My Infinitude is not exclusive but spiritual, and includes the fulness of all spiritual life, eternal love. Think of Me as always communicating life, and love, and power—as always receiving love. Never pronounce the word "God" without recognizing that diversity of reciprocal life which *is* the highest life—the reconciliation of life overflowing and returning, which cannot be without a perfect union of distinct personalities.'

"The Incarnation, if believable, seems to me to throw a strong light on the seeming contradictions of human nature—contradictions which are only brought out into sharper relief by a fuller knowledge of the Creator. The more we acknowledge the greatness of God, the more are we perplexed by contending thoughts as to the nature of man. The knowledge we have gained only humiliates and crushes us, or produces an artificial elation. We either crouch with the highest of purely Jewish minds, or become urbanely self-content with the Pelagian-Unitarian thinkers. We either cry, 'Woe is me! for I am undone, because I am a man of unclean lips; for mine eyes have seen the King, the Lord of hosts!' or we congratulate ourselves that we are, by inherent right, children of God, 'born good,' as Lord Palmerston said, and have no profound need, therefore, of purification at all. The humiliation alone, and the exaltation alone, are alike false to the facts within us and destructive of the true springs of human hope. The 'coal from the altar' which purified Isaiah's lips was a special deliverance from the abject humiliation of Oriental self-abasement—a kind of deliverance which is not universal enough for mankind; and, on the other hand, the persuasion that we ourselves are, in our own right, children of God, is a graver delusion in the other direction. What we want is some universal fountain of divine life within us which shall yet not blind us in any way to the truth that we ourselves are not by our own right children of God, but only become so through One Who is. We need a reconciliation of the fact of the unhealthy egoism of our own individualities, with the equally certain fact of a divine Light struggling with that egoism, and claiming us as true children of God.

"The Incarnation alone helps us adequately to understand ourselves; it reconciles the language of servile humiliation with the language of rightful children. Both are true. The unclean slave and the free child of heaven are both within us. The Incarnation shows us the true Child of God—the filial will which never lost its majesty, which never tasted the impurity of human sin—and so still further abases us; but then it shows Him as the incarnate revelation of that Eternal Son and Word, whose filial light and life can stream into and take possession of us, with power to make us like Himself. The Incarnation alone seems to me adequately to reconcile the contradictory facts of a double nature in man—the separate individuality which has no health of its own, and turns every principle to evil directly it begins to revolve on its own axis—and the divine nature which lends it a true place and true subordination in the kingdom of God. 'We are not,' said Athanasius, 'by *nature* sons of God, but the Son in us makes us so; also, God is not *by nature our* Father, but He is the Father of the Word, dwelling in us; for in Him and through Him we cry, "Abba, Father."' It is obvious that Athanasius uses the word 'nature' here in a much narrower sense than Bishop

Butler. In the largest sense it *is* our true 'nature' to live in and through the Eternal Word. But what Athanasius meant—namely, that not by virtue of anything in our own strict personality or individuality, only by virtue of the divine life engrafted upon that personality or individuality, do we become sons of God—seems to me the very truth which St. John reveals:—'He came unto His own, and His own received Him not; but as many as received Him, to them gave He the power to become sons of God.' This teaching, and this alone, seems to vindicate the divine nature *in* us without leading us into the delusion that it is *of* us."

It is no mere figure of speech to declare that without Christ, understood as He represented Himself and as the Church has conceived Him, humanity is lost. It is without the knowledge of God. It is without the knowledge of itself. It is true that great multitudes have some part of this knowledge who yet do not accept Jesus Christ as the Eternal Son of God, but they would not have it if He had not been the Eternal Son of God and brought this knowledge into the world.

But it is not only the knowledge of God which Christ gives us. It is God. The healing of sin in us, the removal of its burden, the dissipation of its darkness, the sense of pardon and forgiveness,—these things which no man could ever give to us Jesus gave to men when He was here and is giving to men still. And He gave them then and is giving them now because He was able to deal with sin and the soul bowed under sin as no man could deal.

PROFESSOR EDWARD EVERETT HALE'S EXPERIENCE

Perhaps it will help us to read now a part of Professor Hale's account. It confirms the views I have quoted from Mr. Hutton: "In earlier days," writes Mr. Hale, referring especially to John iii:16, "the Gospel of John was without interest to me. That seems to me now very natural. There was comparatively little in it that to me bore the stamp of authenticity, for the characteristic events in the life of Jesus, and the accompanying teaching, found no particular answer in my own experience. I was just as much puzzled as Nicodemus at what was said of being born again. I had no particular sympathy with the unique confidence of the man born blind who had received his sight. I saw very little meaning even in Jesus' words of consolation to Martha when she grieved, though she knew her brother was to rise again at the last day. There is much in the Gospel so beautiful that it will reach all hearts; but a good deal of it will, I think, remain a pretty dark saying to one who had not tried the great experiment of trusting everything to Jesus as a living Saviour, with the expectation of gaining thereby the life that is independent of the conditions of every-day existence, and of the death that must come to all.

"So, if I paid little attention to this passage, or even to the whole Gospel, it was natural enough; it was probably even inevitable. What should this particular text have meant to one whose definite belief was that Jesus was not the only begotten Son of God, but the greatest among many sons; who held that it was not by belief in Jesus that one should be saved, but rather by incorporating into one's life and character the principles of His teaching; who did not readily conceive of any real perishing on the part of those who put their trust elsewhere than in Him? One can see, I believe, that with such a one this text had no great weight, even though it were in the Gospel of John, but on the other hand that the Gospel lost something by having the text in it.

"On the other hand, let it be the case that this passage gains with a given person, say, especial importance from its application to the conditions of mission work in our cities. This, too, is not accidental, but really very characteristic. The text is a fine text for its place; but the place it holds is a pretty typical one, and the reason that it is good where it is, is reason enough for its being good in other very different places. For I suppose we do not think of it as authoritative, but simply as declarative; not as a truth that is true because it is expressed where it is expressed, but a truth that is so to us because it expresses so much that we know. Then we see that these few words say to us that God is not merely a lawgiver, but a Father; that Jesus is not merely an elder brother, but a divine Saviour; that the salvation He offers is open to any one that will avail himself of it; that those who will not take it are turning away from the only possibility of true life; that those who come to Him are thereby beginning upon a life that is independent of the conditions of time or place in this world or any other. All these things, doubtless, are things that one wants to impress on a set of homeless men, hard up or 'down and out,' who come to a mission meeting largely because it is a good warm place on a cold night, and who yet have some pretty definite idea that there is a God, that they have souls, and that somehow or other they will have to make answer to Him for their life here. But these things are only good to impress upon such because these things are also impressed on all who accept Christ as their Saviour. They are put on the wall of a mission room only because written in the hearts of all Christians.

"It is now somewhat more than two years since I was called to acknowledge Jesus Christ as a living Saviour. It was at a revival meeting that I did so, and at the end of that meeting the general advice was given to those who had just made decisions, to read the Gospel of John. I remember at the time thinking the advice was by no means wise or to the point. One will easily see the cause of that idea: the Gospel of John had always seemed to me impractical, mystical, philosophical, by no means such as to be read by any one who did not have already a pretty well grounded faith, and a fairly well developed idea of the essentials of Christian doctrine and life. I did not at that moment appreciate the new spirit with which one would read who had just seen reason to believe that Jesus was the Son of God, and who had in that belief found himself at the beginning of a new life. I did not understand that though the book was written to induce belief, it yet had infinitely more meaning to one who already did believe.

"At any rate, I did not read it with especial care for some time. I did read the Bible with great and new interest; indeed for a great while I could not be interested in anything else, and even now I find no book to compare in interest with it, or with something that explains or illustrates it. Still for various reasons, either because there was so much else to read, or because there was so much else to do, I did not read the Gospel of John with care for some time.

"When I did so, I was surprised to see what a simple, practical, every-day book it was,—how entirely different from my earlier conceptions. Matters which had seemed inexplicable, figurative, exaggerated, or without clear or definite meaning, were, I found, statements of matters of experience that I knew about. Incidents in the lives of those who had come in contact with Jesus in the flesh appeared at once to be, in essentials at least, prototypes of incidents in the lives of those who meet and know Him today in the spirit only. I think Luke vii:36-50 was the first Gospel story that impressed me most forcibly in this way, but among the first was the utterance of the blind man in John ix:25. This experiential character, as it may be called, gave a realizing understanding, not only to the rest of the Bible, but particularly, perhaps, to the Gospel of John, and not only to event or incident, but to much else, as for example, this Golden Text.

"Thus the thought of God as a God of love: I must confess that, in spite of the importance of this element in my father's preaching, it was never a realized element in my own belief. In fact, today, I do not see how God is readily thought of as a God of love, save as He is revealed to us as such by Jesus. As God of law He was to me, but His law was something external, something to a great degree arbitrary, something in fact that I did not like. John in his epistle says that we love God because He first loved us. Others may see in the order of the universe and of human life sufficient evidence of the love of God for humanity. I do not mean that it is not there; but I did not see it till I saw the love of God revealed to us in the life and death and the life everlasting of Jesus. That was a light by which I could see what had been there before, but unseen.

"So with the rest—it would take too long to comment on the whole text—that Jesus is His only begotten Son; that anybody may come to Him; that if one does come, one has life everlasting; that if one does not, one has not that life. All these things mean something to me now, because they are a part of my own experience; because they have become, not announcements of external truth, but expressions of what is the natural order of my existence.

"Jesus said that no one comes to the Father but by Him, that He is the way. It is certainly so."

Every man may have this experience if he will. Whoever will make the experiment will find Christ all that He claimed to be, all that the Church has held Him to be. You too will be able to say, when you make the test, what good Dr. Bonar has said in his hymn:

"I heard the voice of Jesus say,
'Come unto Me and rest;
Lay down, thou weary one, lay down,
Thy head upon My breast.'
I came to Jesus as I was,
Weary and worn and sad,
I found in Him a resting-place,
And He has made me glad.

"I heard the voice of Jesus say,
'Behold I freely give
The living water; thirsty one,
Stoop down and drink, and live.'
I came to Jesus, and I drank
Of that life-giving stream;
My thirst was quenched, my soul revived,
And now I live in Him.

"I heard the voice of Jesus say,
'I am this dark world's light;
Look unto Me, thy morn shall rise,
And all thy day be bright.'
I looked to Jesus and I found
In Him my Star, my Sun;
And in that light of life I'll walk,
Till travelling days are done."

III

WHAT THE DEATH OF CHRIST MEANS TO ME

THERE are some human tragedies in which there is no element of mystery. Or if there be, it is only that the tragedy was so long delayed. But there are other tragedies so deep and dark that their mystery is beyond our comprehension. Of all these the death of Jesus Christ was the deepest and darkest. That the truest friend who ever lived should have been betrayed by one of His own disciples for thirty pieces of silver, with a kiss, in His favourite place of prayer; that the best man in history should have been nailed to a cross between two thieves; that the Saviour of the world should have been murdered by the humanity that He came to save; that He who knew no sin should be made sin and the Prince of Life be humbled to drink the cup of death—this is a mystery so deep and so dark that against the background of it every other mystery seems by comparison clear and comprehensible. This then is a place of beginning. The death of Christ makes almost intelligible to us our own so vastly lesser tragedies.

A few months ago one of our most useful and beloved ministers was called to mourn the death of a brilliant son. The boy had been graduated from one of our best colleges. He had just completed his course in the theological school. He was a remarkable musician and in the evening when he came home his coming was known by the glory of the music as he sat down at the piano always open for his return. A career of richest service seemed to lie open before him. And then one Saturday morning he was stricken with infantile paralysis and on Monday he was gone. A few weeks before, one of our choicest young women missionaries had slipped away in Syria. She was a girl of rare beauty and charm. She had been born in Syria and spoke Arabic as her own tongue. She had had the finest educational training in America and had gone back as a nurse to the mission hospital at Tripoli. Everybody loved her. She was the picture of health and joy. What she could have accomplished no words could adequately express. But a Voice called her and after only a fortnight's illness she was taken from us. And to everyone reading these words mysteries like these have come home. What explanation can we find for them? None, save this. These loved ones must have been needed elsewhere more even than here. And this mystery is as light against the dark background of the death of Christ. If this could have come to Him, if God and God's Son had to meet this, then we can be still about our anguish and loss. There must be a meaning for our tragedies in the vastly deeper meaning of His death.

And that death is a symbol, a sign, even more, it is the supreme act of the struggle of good with evil. There is such a struggle. This was the deep conviction of primitive Christianity. As Paul expressed it, "Put on the whole armour of God, that ye may be able to stand against the wiles of the devil. For our wrestling is not against flesh and blood, but against the principalities, against the powers, against the world-rulers of this darkness, against the spiritual hosts of wickedness in the heavenly places" (Eph. vi:11, 12). The devil was no mere metaphor to the early Christians. They knew him as a real and deadly adversary. It is thus that Peter characterizes him, "Your adversary the devil" (I Peter v:8). James appeals for resistance to him (Jas. iv:7), conceiving him as an enemy who can be put to flight. Both in the experience and in the teaching of Jesus we meet this most real and awful conflict. "Then was Jesus led up of the Spirit into the wilderness to be tempted of the devil" (Matt. iv:1). "And the enemy that sowed them is the devil: and the harvest is the end of the world; and the reapers are angels" (Matt. xiii:39). "Then shall He say also unto them on the left hand, depart from me, ye cursed, into the eternal fire which is prepared for the devil and his angels" (Matt. xxv:41). "And He said unto her, For this saying go thy way; the demon is gone out of thy daughter" (Mark vii:29). "When I was daily with you in the temple, ye stretched not forth your hands against Me: but this is your hour, and the power of darkness" (Luke xxii:53). Only so malign a power could have instigated such a deed of shame and night as the betrayal of Jesus: "And during supper, the devil having already put into the heart of Judas Iscariot, Simon's son, to betray Him" (John xiii:2).

This evil personality appears as Satan in the thought of Paul in his Epistles, of John in The Revelation and of Jesus Himself. "Then saith Jesus unto him, Get thee hence, Satan: for it is written, Thou shalt worship the Lord thy God, and Him only shalt thou serve" (Matt. iv:10). "And if Satan casteth out Satan, he is divided against himself; how then shall his kingdom stand?" (Matt. xii:26). "But He turned, and said unto Peter, Get thee behind me, Satan: thou art a stumbling-block unto me: for thou mindest not the things of God, but the things of men" (Matt. xvi:23). "And He said unto them, I beheld Satan fallen as lightning from heaven" (Luke x:18). "And Satan entered into Judas who was called Iscariot, being of the number of the twelve" (Luke xxii:3). "Simon, Simon, behold, Satan asked to have you, that he might sift you as wheat" (Luke xxii:31). "And after the sop, then entered Satan into him. Jesus therefore saith unto him, What thou doest, do quickly" (John xiii:27). "And these are they by the way side, where the word is sown; and when they have heard, straightway cometh Satan, and taketh away the word which hath been sown in them" (Mark iv:15).

We are discerning again these most deadly realities. As Dr. Adolf Keller writes of contemporary thought in Europe: "We are coming back to the first Christian conception of the world. The world is not plastic material to be easily moulded by Christian influence. There is a hostile demonic element. The Church has to fight stubbornly against principalities and powers for its faith and liberty, for the conversion of the peoples and the spread of the Gospel."

This is a different view from that which has prevailed for the last two or three generations. Under a misleading and fallacious theory transferred to society from biology where it is still unestablished, it was assumed that humanity was, at the worst, neutral stuff to be fashioned with ready responsiveness into goodness and greatness, that there was no inherited taint or evil bias which stood in the way of happy and advancing progress. This was the cheerful faith behind John Morley's Positivism and Mr. Carnegie's great benevolence. In Mr. Carnegie's letter of December 14, 1910, to those whom he first chose as Trustees of the Carnegie Endowment for International Peace he wrote: "When civilized nations enter into such treaties as named, and war is discarded as disgraceful to civilized men, as personal war (duelling) and man-selling and buying (slavery) have been discarded within the wide boundaries of our English-speaking race, the Trustees will please then consider what is the next most degrading remaining evil or evils whose banishment—or what new elevating element or elements if introduced or fostered, or both combined—would most advance the progress, elevation and happiness of man, and so on from century to century without end, my Trustees of each age shall determine how they can best aid man in his upward march to higher and higher stages of development unceasingly; for now we know that man was created, not with an instinct for his own degradation, but imbued with the desire and the power for improvement to which, perchance, there may be no limit short of perfection even here in this life upon earth. Let my Trustees therefore ask themselves from time to time, from age to age, how they can best help man in his glorious ascent onward and upward and to this end devote this fund."

Alas, the problem of human progress is vastly darker and more difficult than this. The forces of deterioration are as powerful in themselves as the forces of advance. Darkness wars against Light. The Gates of Hell seek to bar the purpose of Christ. He came as a Saviour to grapple with the power of disease and death. "Since then the children are sharers in flesh and blood, He also Himself in like manner partook of the same; that through death He might bring to nought him that had the power of death, that is, the devil; and might deliver all them who through fear of death were all their lifetime subject to bondage" (Heb. ii:14, 15).

The death of Christ was the death grapple of God with Evil. It released the life of Christ into humanity, as Dr. Henry Clay Trumbull has set forth in his two great books, *The Blood Covenant* and *The Threshold Covenant*. The second Adam, as Paul argued, undid the deed of the first Adam, yes, much more than undid it: "But not as the trespass, so also is the free gift. For if by the trespass of the one the many died, much more did the grace of God, and the gift by the grace of the one man, Jesus Christ, abound unto the many. And not as through one that sinned, so is the gift: for the judgment came of one unto condemnation, but the free gift came of many trespasses unto justification. For if, by the trespass of the one, death reigned through the one; much more shall they that receive the abundance of grace and of the gift of righteousness reign in life through the one, even Jesus Christ. So then as through one trespass the judgment came unto all men to condemnation; even so through one act of righteousness the free gift came unto all men to justification of life" (Rom. v:15-18).

It seems difficult for some Christians to believe this. Sin to them seems stronger than grace, and Adam in his doing more powerful than Jesus in His undoing. Dr. Trumbull deals with this in his remarkable little book, *Our Misunderstood Bible*.

"I longed to believe that as much for good was wrought to the race by the Second Adam as had been wrought for evil by the First Adam. I had been brought up to believe that Christ was more, not less, than Adam in both His work and His influence. If I had been mistaken as to this I must learn Bible truth all over again. Then I newly turned to the Bible for light on this subject. I saw that the Scriptures left no doubt on this point. The pervasive, cleansing power of Christ for good was every way greater than that of evil wrought to the race by Adam. In consequence of this, 'where sin abounded (through Adam) grace (through Christ) did abound more exceedingly' (Rom. v:20). This gave me new light and love in my better understanding of the work and grace of Christ.

"From this new starting-point I studied the Scriptures with added profit and gratitude, finding them fully consistent with the, to me, freshly-disclosed truth, in preference to the old error, by whomsoever taught or held. It proved to me that there is a new covenant of grace, bringing light and life to such as me and mine. And now I am confident that through God's love in Jesus Christ every child of Adam's descendants comes into being as free from guilt and its condemnation as Adam was created. Of course there are all the added tendencies toward sin, and all the physical and mental weaknesses which grow out of wrong habits indulged by successive generations of human parents; but spiritually every human child starts as free and with as much ground for hope as Adam started. Until, therefore, a child has deliberately and wilfully chosen to sin he is not a sinner, and does not stand under condemnation.

"As to this precious truth, I am now, and I long have been, as confident as of the truth that Jesus Christ is the Saviour. How much more God's love seems to me since God's word discloses to me this truth! And how much more is the recognized work of Christ, and how much vaster is the scope of His redemption, than when limited and perverted by the pernicious errors of human illogical and unscriptural dogmas under which I was brought up—or kept down!" [1]

But how does Christ deal with our need, with the malign forces of evil in us? By His life, answers Paul. "For if, while we were enemies," he writes, "we were reconciled to God through the death of His Son,

[1] H. C. Trumbull, *Our Misunderstood Bible* (Sunday School Times Co.).

much more, being reconciled, shall we be saved by His life" (Rom. v:10). His death was the gift of His life. The blood of His Cross was His outpoured life.

All illustrations and analogies are inadequate to cover the meaning of this death and its release of life, but one experience may help. Some years ago a friend who was a medical missionary in Africa was attacked by a strange disease which neither he nor any of his associates could diagnose. It involved excruciating suffering, but neither he nor they knew of any proper treatment for it. At last in despair he was put on a ship and sent home to America. He was taken at once to one of the best hospitals in New York and put under the ablest medical and surgical care. His case aroused the greatest interest. The hospital staff gathered about him day after day studying his case and seeking to discover some hopeful course of dealing with it. At last one of the younger consultants said, "Well, we are not getting anywhere, and the man is suffering unbearably, and no man can stand such suffering long. We don't know what this disease is, and accordingly we don't know what to prescribe for it. But it looks like this other disease which we do know. Can we do any better, we certainly can't do worse, than treat it as though it were this other disease, which it is not but which it resembles?" They all agreed that there was no better course, and accordingly they proceeded to use the serum which they would have used for the other disease. In three weeks the man was well, and one day he came down to our offices in the picture of health and told us his story. "When that serum was injected into me," he said, "I was lying on my bed in anguish. Every particle of my body seemed to be in pain. It was as though an army of implacable enemies had taken possession of me and were trying to torture and destroy me. Then the serum was poured into me. It was as though a new army had been released to wage war with the other army with my body as the battle-ground. The war began at my feet. I could feel the new army begin to drive back the old. Along the battle front it was indescribable anguish. Behind it there was ineffable peace. Slowly the warfare moved right up my body. When it reached my heart I wondered how much longer I could endure, and when it came up into my brain I thought the very roof of my head would blow off. But that was the last. The benign allies who had come to my relief had won the battle. New life had come to me. It was as a new creation. And I lay on my bed in heavenly blessedness and peace."

This is only a poor and partial figure, but it is valid and true. It is not the whole meaning of the Atonement, but it is a blessed part of its meaning in personal experience. "The mystery of iniquity" (II Thess. ii:7) was met and matched in the death of Christ by "the mystery of godliness" (I Tim. iii:16; I Cor. ii:7; Eph. iii:3, 4; vi:19). "The Man of Sin" (II Thess. ii:3) was vanquished by the Man of Righteousness (Rom. v:17), the true Man of God (I Tim. iii:16), the Man Christ Jesus (I Tim. ii:5). And in us the power of this iniquity and of the Man of Sin from whom it emanates is broken by the power of the Son of God. A new life, released by the death and flowing from the life of Christ, supplants the old life in us and we go forth, as my medical missionary friend went forth, new creatures (II Cor. v:17; Gal. vi:15). This is the glorious doctrine of the New Testament about the death of Christ:

"We were buried therefore with Him through baptism into death: that like as Christ was raised from the dead through the glory of the Father, so we also might walk in newness of life. For if we have become united with Him in the likeness of His death, we shall be also in the likeness of His resurrection; knowing this, that our old man was crucified with Him, that the body of sin might be done away, that so we should no longer be in bondage to sin; for He that hath died is justified from sin. But if we died with Christ, we believe that we shall also live with Him; knowing that Christ being raised from the dead dieth no more; death no more hath dominion over Him. For the death that He died, He died unto sin once: but the life that He liveth, He liveth unto God. Even so reckon ye also yourselves to be dead unto sin, but alive unto God in Christ Jesus" (Rom. vi:4-11).

Our minds and hearts rest in the simple, sure language of the Bible in these things. There are some who prefer the language of theology and speak of the substitutionary or vicarious atonement of Christ. Nothing is clearer than the fact that Christ died for us, but not one of these three great words is found in the New Testament. The word "atonement" is used once in the King James Version in Romans v:2, but neither of the other words can be found, and the Revised Version changes "atonement" in this verse in Romans to "reconciliation," which is the correct translation of the Greek word used by Paul, which he uses also in II Corinthians v:18, 19, where, as in Romans v:11, it refers not to a change in God's attitude toward man but to a change in man's attitude toward God. We fall back on the glorious simple teaching of the New Testament: "Christ also suffered for sins once, the righteous for the unrighteous, that He might bring us to God" (I Peter iii:18). He did not need to die in order to bring God to us. He had already done that in the Incarnation. "He that hath seen Me hath seen the Father." "And the Word was made flesh, and dwelt among us, and we beheld His glory, the glory as of the only begotten of the Father, full of grace and truth" (John i:14). It was not the death of Christ that won the love of God. It was the love of God that gave Christ to die (John iii:16). "But God commendeth His love toward us, in that, while we were yet sinners, Christ died for us" (Rom. v:8).

The death of Christ is not only the mystery which gives intelligibility to our human tragedies, and the supreme act in the struggle of the Powers of Darkness and of Death with the Prince of Light and Life, it is also the great event which brings God fully into our human experience. "I have lost my son, my dear son," we say in our human anguish as we bow down over our dead. And then we say softly and with a deep wonder, "And God also. He lost His Son, His dear Son. I suffer. But God Himself went through this. He suffered, too. How He must have suffered!" There have been those who have denied that God could suffer. But a God who could not suffer could not be the God and Father of our Lord Jesus Christ, who notes the sparrow's fall and counts the hairs on the heads of His children and carries their names graven on the palms of His hands (Isa. xlix:6). Our God is not one to whom "no sound of human sorrow mounts to mar His sacred, everlasting calm." If David in the little room over the gate could have waited in eager expectancy for word of Absalom and could have sobbed out his heart there over that wastrel and ingrate, "O Absalom, how often would I have died for thee, O Absalom, my son, my son," if Jesus could have wept over the city that rejected and crucified Him, "O Jerusalem, Jerusalem," what must have gone on in the heart of God as He looked down on His own dear, obedient, sinless Son suffering on His cross! The death of Jesus brings God down into our human experience. "Yes," we say, "God has shared our lot with us. We have lost our son. God also lost His."

And the death of Jesus not only brings God into human experience. It has carried our human experience into God. We dare be as bold as the truth of the Gospel here. God, we very reverently say, knows what pain and death mean now since the experience of them has been carried into God by Christ.

"And there He sits this moment man and God
Strong as a God, flesh-hearted as a man,
And all the uncreated light confronts
With eyelids that have known the touch of tears."

This is the doctrine of the New Testament, which says of Christ in God what could not be said of God before the Incarnation and Death of Christ:

"Since then the children are sharers in flesh and blood, He also Himself in like manner partook of the same; that through death He might bring to nought him that had the power of death, that is, the devil; and might deliver all them who through fear of death were all their lifetime subject to bondage. For verily not to angels doth He give help, but He giveth help to the seed of Abraham. Wherefore it behooved Him in all things to be made like unto His brethren, that He might become a merciful and faithful high priest in things pertaining to God, to make propitiation for the sins of the people. For in that He Himself hath suffered being tempted, He is able to succour them that are tempted" (Heb. ii:14-18). "Having then a great high priest, who hath passed through the heavens, Jesus the Son of God, let us hold fast our confession. For we have not a high priest that cannot be touched with the feeling of our infirmities; but one that hath been in all points tempted like as we are, yet without sin. Let us therefore draw near with boldness unto the throne of grace, that we may receive mercy, and may find grace to help us in time of need" (Heb. iv:14-16).

The death of Christ has given us a different God, one who has shared our human experience and who is and knows what even God would not have been and could not have known but for the death of His dear Son.

And the death of Christ not only carries our human experience forward into God, it also throws light back on the deepest and most mysterious experience in the earthly life of Christ, namely, His agony in the Garden of Gethsemane. What was the meaning of that experience? The cup which He prayed might be taken from Him is often understood as His approaching death on the Cross, just as it is suggested that when, a short time before, the visit of the Greeks brought before His mind all that His mission involved, He prayed to be spared: "Father, save me from this hour." As Dr. James Stalker even has written in his nearly perfect little *Life of Jesus Christ:* "Some have hesitated to attribute to Him aught of that shrinking from death which is natural to man; but surely without good reason. It is an instinct perfectly innocent; and perhaps the very fact that His bodily organism was pure and perfect may have made it stronger in Him than it is in us. Remember how young He was—only three-and-thirty—the currents of life were powerful in Him: He was full of the instincts of action. To have these strong currents rolled back and the light and warmth of life quenched in the cold waters of death must have been utterly repugnant to Him." But recall Paul's words in Acts xx:22-24; xxi:13, and consider how many of His disciples have never felt this shrinking but have gone joyfully, even gaily to their death in His name and for His sake, men, women and even children.

> "A noble army, men and boys, the matron and the maid
> Around the Saviour's throne rejoice, in robes of white arrayed.
> They climbed the steep ascent of heaven through peril, toil and pain."

They counted it great joy to follow in the footsteps of their Master who, never shrinking or flinching, "for the joy that was set before Him endured the cross, despising the shame." Even under the reminder of His testing which the visit of the Greeks brought to Him He did not shrink. "And what shall I say. Father, save Me from this hour? But for this cause came I unto this hour. Father, glorify Thy name."

And so it cannot be that in Gethsemane Jesus was shrinking from death or drawing back from the Cross. What He feared in Gethsemane was not death on the Cross, but death before the Cross. The burden of the sin of the world that He was bearing was proving too heavy for Him. It seemed that it would crush Him then and there in the garden before ever He had finished His work upon the Cross, and He prayed earnestly not for escape from the Cross, but for strength to go forward to the Cross. What else can be the meaning of the passage in the Epistle to the Hebrews? "Who in the days of His flesh, having offered up prayers and supplications with strong crying and tears unto Him that was able to save Him from death, and having been heard for His godly fear" (Heb. v:7). To what experience in Jesus' life but Gethsemane can these words refer? If He prayed to be spared the Cross, though submitting to it if it was God's will, then He was not heard, as the writer of the Hebrews says He was. As indeed the very record of Gethsemane shows: "Father, if Thou be willing, remove this cup from Me: nevertheless, not my will, but Thine, be done. And there appeared unto Him an angel from heaven, strengthening Him" (Luke xxii:42, 43).

This understanding makes Gethsemane intelligible and glorious. This is no fanciful interpretation and we can fortify it with a passage from an old Scotch book long out of print, William Anderson's *Filial Honour of God:*

"The reply which those with whom I now most reluctantly contend make to the question, or rather exclamation, What were Paul's sufferings compared with those of Christ! is virtually that they were no less, or rather much the same; that death threatened them both in forms equally fearful—in the case of Christ in the form of being crucified, for the gratification of the malice of Jewish Priests; in that of Paul, in the form of being beheaded for the bloodthirstiness of Nero; but that Paul, in the immediate prospect of his death, was composed, yea triumphant, saying, 'I am now ready to be offered; henceforth there is laid up for me a crown of righteousness;' whereas Christ, in the prospect of his, was agonized with terror, and prayed importunately to be saved from it, if possible. It is painful to write, and I hope painful for many to read, what is so discrediting to our Lord.

"When those who make the injurious representation explain that it was not a common crucifixion which He deprecated, but one of peculiar horror; because in it He would be subjected to the bearing of the curse of the sin of the whole world, or at least of the whole elect part of it, What, I ask, do they mean? Is it that He feared that scope would be given to the malice of the Priests, the prototypes of Popish Inquisitors, in refining, somehow or other, the torture of crucifixion? Or, that He feared that Divine Justice might demand more than an ordinary prolongation of suffering, and for that end might supernaturally sustain Him in life, under more agony than the human constitution usually requires for its extinction? I do not ask such questions with the least of a feeling of burlesque. Both the cause, and the character of the men whom I question forbid this. Let them tell us something, though it be ever so general and undefined, of the reason wherefore Christ was agonized in the prospect of death, when Paul was composed. It is no answer to say that the causes of the deaths were different, and that the cause of that of Christ, being the weightier, it gave reason to apprehend a more dreadful issue; for there was no room for imagining fears: both of the deaths were distinctly specified, and they were equally dreadful. I therefore repeat the demand, Will they give us any plausible explanation which sustains the honour of our great Exemplar—of Paul encountering his death with little or no perturbation of mind, when Christ anticipated His with a fear which produced perspiration of blood? They never will, so long as they imagine that it was the fear of crucifixion by which Christ was agonized in Gethsemane.

"But, dismissing all comparison with the case of Paul, I go on to remark that, how much soever they may magnify Christ's reasons for regarding the Cross in such near prospect with horror, the fact will remain, that according to their views He prayed for deliverance from drinking the prepared cup of that Cross's anguish, if it were possible. It is this that amazes me especially, in the teaching of pious and learned men. Observe, they admit that, whether through the illumination of his own Divine nature, or that of the Spirit of His Father, the human soul of Christ was clearly convinced that in order to the fulfilment of His mission He must suffer a violent death, and that specially by being 'lifted up' on the Cross; and yet they represent Him as praying that He might be delivered from it if possible. Is not this amazing interpretation indeed?—to represent Him praying for that, as being possibly possible, which He was sure was impossible—for that as being possibly agreeable to his Father's will, the contrary of which He knew his Father's will had from eternity decreed—for that which, were it granted, He distinctly knew would be a complete abandonment of the enterprise of the world's salvation? The amazement is only heightened by the attempted explanation. It is, that the natural shrinking of Christ's humanity, in view of the impending sufferings of crucifixion, prevailed for a moment to make Him pray for deliverance; but that He presently recovered his fortitude! Now, though this alleged succumbing to natural fear had been momentary, which it was not—for He prayed in the same manner a second and a third time at considerable intervals—though it had been strictly momentary, what could have been said in justification of the feelings and expressions of that moment? To represent the human nature of Christ as shrinking in the near view of that cross of torment discredits neither His fortitude nor faith. It would not increase my admiration of the character of Paul to be assured that he did not shrink at the sight of the headsman with his axe; but it is one thing to shrink in the sight of impending suffering and utter exclamations of woe, and quite another to desire an escape when duty clearly demands submission to it; and something very different to pray to be delivered from it, when He who prays knows that deliverance is impossible. Yet, this is what many represent Christ to have done. I may not mention in connection with his Name what this imputes to Him. I only say it is amazing that 'in the house of His friends,' He should be wounded by the imputation.

"The amazement rises yet higher, when the difficulty, if difficulty there be in the case, is so easily explained. I therefore vehemently, and on behalf of Christ, indignantly deny that His prayer was either momentarily or conditionally deprecatory of His being made to drink tomorrow of the prepared cup of the expiatory sufferings of the Cross; and contend that it was deprecatory only of the prolongation of His drinking of that cup of mental anguish which was already, that dark night, being administered to Him. What were all the ingredients of that cup no man may attempt satisfactorily to explain. That horror of the Cross was one of them is most probable; but if so it was not the Cross from which He prayed to be delivered, but the present overwhelming horror of it.

"Independently of direction from any other quarter we might have concluded, with certainty, from the evangelical narratives themselves that it was the cup of mental tribulation, which He was presently drinking, that was the object of his deprecatory prayer. I, for one, could not for a moment have entertained the imagination (to be afterwards dispossessed of it), that when He was yet warm, so to speak, from instituting an ordinance to be observed by His Church in all ages till He returned in His glory, as commemorative of His approaching death, He should yet have commenced to pray for escape from that death, with strong crying and tears; and that, too, after having mocked at Peter's self-confidence, when he protested that he would not succumb, even momentarily, to the natural shrinking from death. But without any such prepossession of mind against the possibility of the Cross itself being the object of His deprecation, the narrative at its very commencement determines what the cup is, and discloses the Saviour drinking of it: 'My soul is exceeding sorrowful, even unto death.' It is this agony of sorrow which forms the subject of the whole passage—as being the contents of the cup—as being that from which He was delivered. To represent the agonies of the Cross as being the contents of the deprecated cup is not only morally objectionable in the highest degree, but evinces a lack of exegetical scholarship, in substituting a supposed cause of the sorrow for the sorrow itself, which is pointedly set forth as the subject of the narrative,—a substitution which has produced, in the attempted expositions of those who make it, a jumble of self-contradictions, and what is worse, most injurious imputations to the character of our Lord.

"Although, however, there is enough in the evangelical

narratives themselves of Matthew, Mark, and Luke, to convince us that the deprecated cup was that of present mental agony, and not that of the approaching pains of crucifixion, yet, when error prevails so much we cannot dispense with referring to the inspired testimony of the Apostle as given in Hebrews v:7: 'Who in the days of His flesh, when He had offered up prayers and supplications with strong crying and tears unto Him that was able to save Him from death; and was heard in that He feared.'

"In adducing this evidence we are, in the first instance, met by the denial of Macknight, that the Apostle refers in these words to the scene of Gethsemane at all. His argument is, that whereas the Apostle represents Him as having prayed for and received deliverance from death, He presented no such prayer that night; for this eminent critic contends as vehemently as I have done, that to suppose Him to have prayed in fear of the Cross 'would be to degrade His character infinitely' (*Harmony,* sect. CXXXIV). He therefore 'conjectures' that the praying with strong crying and tears, spoken of by Paul, refers to some incident in Christ's life which none of the evangelists have recorded; and of which the Apostle was informed either by tradition or direct inspiration; and that His resurrection from the dead was that for which He prayed, and in which He was answered. Is not this strange conjecturing for one deservedly in high repute for his many excellences as an expositor, and worth whole colleges of German fancy-critics? What! No threatening of death in the Gethsemane scene, from which our Lord could pray to be delivered! when He began to be sorrowful, and very heavy, and sore amazed, and said, 'My soul is exceedingly sorrowful, even unto death,' and when He fell on His face praying in agony for deliverance, and when His sweat was as it were great drops of blood falling down to the ground! Even according to these expressions could death be more imminent? But Dr. Doddridge, with good cause, complains that 'the words which our translators use here are very flat, and fall vastly short of the emphasis of these terms in which the Evangelists describe the awful scene.' Especially that translated 'very heavy' signifies 'overwhelmed with anguish.' What greater nearness to death, through mental suffering, could any one reasonably demand to warrant applying to the case the words of the Apostle, that He prayed for deliverance to Him who was able to 'save from death?' Almost all other expositors express themselves to the effect that Christ must have felt as if He would die, were the mental agony prolonged. And Macknight himself says, 'His human nature being now burdened beyond measure, He found it necessary to retire and pray, that if it was possible, or consistent with the salvation of the world, He might be delivered from the sufferings which were then lying on Him' (*Harmony,* sect. XXXIV). I therefore dismiss the 'conjecture' as unworthy of the honoured name of the dreamer—by few honoured so much as by him who laments and censures the temporary hallucination.

"Having established what has been almost the universal opinion in all ages of the Church that Hebrews v:7 refers to the scene in Gethsemane, on its authority I argue, that Christ was delivered from that death which He deprecated; and that that could not be the prospective death of the Cross, since He was not delivered from it, but the present imminent death, through mental agony, whatever may have been its causes, from which He was delivered. There is a difference among critics about the precise meaning of the words of the original, translated in the common version 'was heard in that He feared.' But all agree that they signify that His prayer was answered. It does not appear, but it does not much affect the great question, whether the Apostle refers particularly to the mission of the angel to strengthen Him (Luke xxii:43), or generally to the manner in which His subsequent conduct indicated that He had been delivered from the anguish of soul, extruding bloody sweat, which made Him feel that He must presently die, unless He were relieved. Why, instead of deprecating the Cross, He prayed that He might be spared for it."[2]

Let us go on to note once again that the death of Christ reveals both the limitlessness and the limited-

---

[2] William Anderson, *Filial Honour of God,* pp. 145-153 (Hodder and Stoughton, London).

ness of God. There is an outworn cavil that God is either not a God of love or not a God of power. If He could save everyone and will not, He is not a God of love. If He would save everyone and cannot, He is not a God of power. The answer is simple. God's love is limitless, but not His power. The Cross shows His limitless love, but there are some things that the Cross of Christ shows are beyond His power. On the one hand is God's boundless love and goodness revealed in the Cross. The great words of the Gospel emphasized by the death of Christ were "all" and "uttermost" and "whole world" and "every man." "For the love of Christ constraineth us; because we thus judge, that one died for all, therefore all died" (II Cor. v:14). "Who gave Himself a ransom for all; the testimony to be borne in its own times" (I Tim. ii:6). "One God and Father of all, who is over all, and through all, and in all" (Eph. iv:6). "He that spared not His own Son, but delivered Him up for us all, how shall He not also with Him freely give us all things?" (Rom. viii:32). "Jesus, knowing that the Father had given all things into His hands, and that He came forth from God, and goeth unto God" (John xiii:5). "Wherefore also He is able to save to the uttermost them that draw near unto God through Him, seeing He ever liveth to make intercession for them" (Heb. vii:25). "And He said unto them, go ye into all the world, and preach the gospel to the whole creation" (Mark xvi:15). "But ye shall receive power, when the Holy Spirit is come upon you: and ye shall be my witnesses both in Jerusalem, and in all Judea and Samaria, and unto the uttermost part of the earth" (Acts i:8). "And He is the propitiation for our sins; and not for ours only, but also for the whole world" (I John ii:2). "There was the true light, even the light which lighteth every man, coming into the world" (John i:9). "But I would have you know, that the head of every man is Christ; and the head of the woman is the man; and the head of Christ is God" (I Cor. xi:3). "Whom we proclaim, admonishing every man and teaching every man in all wisdom, that we may present every man perfect in Christ" (Col. i:28). "But we behold Him who hath been made a little lower than the angels, even Jesus, because of the suffering of death crowned with glory and honour, that by the grace of God He should taste of death for every man" (Heb. ii:9).

The Cross showed that there were no bounds to the love of God. The article in the Apostles' Creed, "He descended into hell," may be a difficult article to understand. When was our Lord in hell? Did He not with His last breath lay His Spirit in His Father's hands? Was not His last sure confidence in His prayer, "Now come I to Thee"? Did He not say to the dying thief, "Today thou shalt be with me in Paradise"? And yet the declaration of the Creed is the sure and blessed affirmation of the "love that will not let us go" and that will follow us to the uttermost. The Psalmist rejoiced in this: "If I ascend up into heaven, Thou art there: if I make my bed in Sheol, behold, Thou art there. If I take the wings of the morning, and dwell in the uttermost parts of the sea; even there shall Thy hand lead me, and Thy right hand shall hold me" (Psa. cxxxix:8-10).

The Cross is the pledge of God's love to us. "For God so loved the world, that He gave His only begotten Son, that whosoever believeth on Him should not perish, but have eternal life" (John iii:16). "He that spared not His own Son, but delivered Him up for us all, how shall He not also with Him freely give us all things?" (Rom. viii:32).

But the death of Christ reveals also the twofold limitations of God—the limitations set by our obduracy and the self-limitations set by His own love. It was over the first of these that Jesus wept: "O Jerusalem, Jerusalem, that killeth the prophets, and stoneth them that are sent unto her! how often would I have gathered thy children together, even as a hen gathereth her own brood under her wings, and ye would not! Behold, your house is left unto you desolate: and I say unto you, ye shall not see me, until ye shall say, blessed is He that cometh in the name of the Lord" (Matt. xiii:34, 35). "And when He drew nigh, He saw the city and wept over it, saying, If thou hadst known in this day, even thou, the things which belong unto peace! but now they are hid from thine eyes" (Luke xix:41, 42). If we lose God and our lives it is not of God's ordering: "The Lord is not slack concerning His promise, as some count slackness; but is longsuffering to youward, not wishing that any should perish, but that all should come to repentance" (II Peter iii:9).

Our limits to God's goodwill for us are our shame. But the self-limits which God has set for Himself and which are revealed in the death of Christ are His glory. "He emptied Himself." "He saved others. Himself He could not save." In life and in death Jesus Christ had His limitations. The Christian faith hesitates to use such words; it frightens us to say that the Son of God, "very God of very God," as we believe Him to have been, should have thus hedged Himself in with limitation. And yet such a phrase is only a synonym for the Incarnation. If God was to appear in flesh at all, it must be at some time and in some place; He must be willing to come out of the infinite into space, and out of the eternal into time, and to enmesh Himself in the physical limitations of our human life.

It is not to be denied that many find difficulty in this thought. They say that it is unintelligible, or they say that it is unworthy. It seems inconceivable that God should or could thus have hedged Himself in within the narrow boundaries of our human life, and impossible of thought that the Infinite should thus have laid aside His infinity and have taken on Him the form of a man.

But what God is it Whose incarnation is unintelligible to us? The very ideas of God which make it difficult for us to conceive of the Incarnation, were given us through the Incarnation. We believe in the kind of a God Whom it is hard to conceive as having come in human flesh, just because God did come once in human flesh and revealed Himself to our hearts. And as for its being unworthy, is not precisely the opposite true? Consider the significance of the fact that while men everywhere, in all countries, fear God, no men but Christians love Him, that only those who believe that God once came here and lived among men a man's life dare to love God as a Father and a Friend. All the child verses that open up to us the real secret of the Incarnation reveal to us also how dearly we love God just because He did come in Jesus. Is it not this very thought of God as having once been a little child that makes us dare to love Him? As Bushnell used to say, whatever intellectual difficulties surround a belief in the Trinity, our heart needs God the Father, and our heart needs Christ the Son. No, it was the limitations that surrounded God in Jesus Christ that make God intelligible to us and that make God dear to us.

But it is not of these limitations of Jesus that I speak here. It is rather of those moral self-limitations by which Jesus Christ hedged in and conditioned His life, and which constitute, in a sense, the very glory of the life of the Son of God on earth. The great passage of Scripture that describes alike both of these sets of limitations in the life of our Lord is in Philippians:

"Have this mind in you, which was also in Christ Jesus: Who, being in the form of God, counted not equality with God a prize to be jealously retained, but made Himself of no reputation, and took upon Him the form of a servant; and being found in fashion as a man, He humbled Himself, and became obedient unto death, even the death of the cross. Wherefore God also hath highly exalted Him, and given Him the name which is above every name."

Into the fathomless mysteries of all that is involved here it is not necessary that we should try to penetrate, but we may mark the beauty and splendour of the life of Jesus Christ as revealed in the way He thus deliberately chose for Himself a host of narrowing limitations to His life which we can understand.

We see Jesus beginning to do this in His temptation. What was the significance of the temptation, but that Jesus Christ was confronted there with the inducement to accomplish His ends by the use of what to Him seemed illegitimate means, in what to Him seemed an illegitimate time? If that was the temptation of our Lord, how wonderfully characteristic it was of the Lamb of God, as Seeley says, that He resisted it, and how sublime was the self-restraint by which He was able to do it! One Who conceived Himself born for universal monarchy, as Seeley says, Who felt within Himself the power to achieve by supernatural might the end that was on His heart, deliberately refused to attain His ends in that way, preferred to found His government on the consent rather than upon the fears of men, deliberately decided to entrust Himself with all His terrible purity and superiority defenceless among men, pursued that as a policy, although finally it resulted in the utter apparent failure of His life, and was thereby seated at last upon a throne, where He has been now for nigh two thousand years, and from which He rules the lives of men with a power never dreamed of by any legislator, and more glorious even than was predicted in any of the prophecies in reference to the Messiah. The very significance of the temptation was this: Jesus Christ steadfastly limited Himself there as to the methods that He would use; and as to the time in which He would be content to work out His design, and He cut off by one sheer blow thus in the wilderness well nigh the whole under half of life.

Through all our Lord's earthly life we see the manifestation of this same divinely human self-limitation and restraint. We see it in His teaching. He had many things to say that He never said. The silences of Christ are as significant as His speech. Many, many times when He was on the edge of lifting the veil and giving further revelation to His disciples, as the account of His last night's interview with them only too sadly illustrates, He discovered that the time had not come, and we can see Him drop the veil again with a sort of deep pathos and sadness.

We see it constantly in the things that He did and the things that He did not do. In his sonnet on Christ's self-restraint, Trench is describing what is so significant in Him in His self-limitation of His acts:

> "He might have reared a palace at a word
> Who sometimes had not where to lay His head.
> Time was when He Who nourished crowds with bread
> Would not one meal unto Himself afford.
> He healed another's scratch; His own side bled,
> Side, feet and hands with cruel piercings gored.
> Twelve legions girded with angelic sword
> Stood at His beck, the scorned and buffeted.
> Oh, wonderful the wonders left undone,
> And not less wonderful than those He wrought!
> Oh, self-restraint, surpassing human thought,
> To have all power, yet be as having none!
> Oh, self-denying love that thought alone
> For needs of others, never for Its own!"

I do not wonder that in one of the most striking of the many books that have been written about Jesus Christ, however inadequate we may believe it to have been, Professor Seeley, in *Ecco Homo,* singled this out as the supreme characteristic of His life, namely, that it was not the beauty of His doctrine, it was not the winsomeness of His command to love, it was not the attractiveness of His personality, it was not the marvel of His miracles that won for Jesus Christ the love of those who attached themselves to Him; it was the inimitable unity in which all these things bound themselves together. It lay in this: that He, Whose power and Whose greatness were shown by His miracles to be so overwhelming, steadfastly refused to use that power for Himself, walked among men as one of them, healed their sick and comforted their sorrowing, offered Himself to their need, taught them how to love one another, bore with absolute patience a perfect hail-storm of terrible calumny, and then when His enemies grew fiercer still, met their fiercer onslaughts with perfect patience, and at last, while His disciples looked on dumbfounded with astonishment, met His death of torture, still refusing to use in His own behalf a power which He conceived He held solely for the advantage of others. It was this: the sublime combination in Jesus Christ of greatness and self-sacrifice, His divine condescension, the cross of Jesus Christ, that power in Him which made it possible for Him to save others and made it impossible in Him to save Himself.

It is easy to discover in many small ways this self-limitation of Jesus Christ's life. We behold Him every day surrendering His rights. There are men who think it lies in the nature of a right that it is to be exercised and not surrendered. It did not appear so to Jesus. He did not conceive that because He possessed a right, therefore it was incumbent upon Him to use it. I have a right to keep my seat in the street car if I wish when an old woman with a little child gets in and stands. I have a right also to waive my right. I have a right to do this or that, if I want to; I have a right also to refrain from doing it. It does not follow that because men have rights, therefore men are under obligation to use their rights. As President Woolsey used to say, it lies in the very nature of a right that it creates an obligation in each man who believes himself to possess it to determine in the light of high principle whether the time for its exercise has come. And as we look at the life of our Lord, we behold Him from the beginning to the end shearing off His rights. The Incarnation itself was a gigantic surrender of right, as Dr. B. B. Warfield used to argue; the whole life of Christ was a subjugation to wrong and a waiving of His rights. We see this in the way in which He deliberately limited Himself to devotion to the right and cut off from His life at once all those liberties that lay in the possible devotion of life to wrong principle. Christ chose for Himself deliberately the moral limitation and narrowing of life to the ends that are right, and we cannot approach Christ without feeling this, a new tone in the air, a tightening of the cords, a closing up of the gaps in life. We know that now, at last, we have come into the presence of One unlike everybody else, One Who had made it positively impossible for Himself to do a great many of those things that other men count tolerable in their lives. He found the glory of His life in these moral incapacities, and we draw from this the great lesson that, after all, it is moral inability for wrong as well as moral capacity for right that is the secret of moral power.

This is the very core of true religion. This is one thing that separates our religion from all other religions in the world. It does not matter which one of them we take to compare with it. Let it be Hinduism. What is the supreme distinction between Hinduism and our faith but just this: that our religion is a religion of limitations and Hinduism is a religion without limitations? In *The Imitation of Sree Krishna* the question is asked, Which would be the worthier idea of God, a god who is able both to tell the truth and to lie, or a god who could only tell the truth? Would not the greater and more glorious god be the god who could both tell the truth and lie? [3] Hinduism lacks those

---

[3] "Conceive a man who is trying his utmost to fly from vice to its opposite pole, virtue; imagine also a being to whom heat and cold, virtue and vice, are the same: and you will find that the latter is infinitely superior to the former. The one is the infinite, the other is the finite; the one is the absolute, the other is the relative."—(From preface to *The Imitation of Sree Krishna*, compiled by S. C. Mukopadhaya, M.A.)

limitations of life to the right and the pure which constitute the very essence of the Christian faith. What limitations it has are not so much moral as social—limitations designed to secure, not the promotion of service, but the preservation of privilege; limitations not only not moral, but sometimes positively immoral. Our religion sets itself off against every other, and the higher a man's conception of it, the more definitely it sets itself off by the iron rigidity of the limitations with which it surrounds itself.

And this is the law of this world in which we live also. Limitation is the secret of power. This air that is moving freely all around us now we might condense, if we could, and multiply its power a million fold. We spread a stream out over the fields and it is impotent; we crowd it into a narrow channel and it has power. The laws of moral life are the laws of nature, too. In the moral life, in one aspect, it is inability and not largeness and range that constitutes power; narrowness and not breadth. It is so in our thinking and in our search after truth. In Mr. Leslie Stephen's *History of English Thought in the Eighteenth Century,* the complaint throughout is just the complaint of all men who have tried to write the history of human thought, namely, that men will not be as narrow as the truth. They try to live in the realm of what is false as well as in the realm of what is true, and they are not willing to shut out of the range of their life the error and the imposition and the deception, and to wall themselves in solely to what is true. What is the search after truth but the worship of narrowness, the steady exclusion of every hypothesis until at last we have come down to the rigid, the unyielding, exclusive truth?

It is so in love. The power of love is not found in unlimited license. It is found in the limitation of affection to what is close and personal and distinct. The power of human history has not resided in general benevolence or in the distribution of a general charity over life; it has lain, as Dr. Trumbull has proven in his book on *Friendship,* in that master passion which has bound individual souls together. We do not believe in free love; we believe in the mystical union of duality of souls, and the power of affection and true feeling lies just where the power of intellect lies, in excluding everything that is false and outside the walls, while we pass in where the truth of love abides.

It is so in all service. The men who have weighed in the world and who have accomplished anything have not been the men who have tried everything. "This one thing I do," said Paul. "My meat," said One greater than Paul, "is to do the will of Him Who sent Me, and to finish His work." True narrowness and not false breadth, whether in thought, or feeling, or service, is the secret of power in the moral life. This is true paradox.

The Son of God limited Himself and became the Son of Man. The Son of God who was the Son of Man died for us on His Cross. He saved others. Himself He could not save because He would not. That was one limitation. He laid down His power. With what result? He had a right to lay it down and He had a right to take it again. He who had no power was the same who had all power. He could not save Himself. Even so. And therefore it came that His self-limitation of the Cross shattered the limitation of the Grave. "Because it was not possible that He should be holden of death" (Acts ii:24).

Lastly the death of Christ is the fact in history, the great objective deed, which, completed by the Resurrection, is the basis of Christian salvation both as faith and as experience. Salvation is something done for us, not by us. As Dr. Trumbull says in *Our Misunderstood Bible* in comment on the words of Paul about working out our own salvation (Phil. ii:12):

"If there is one passage in the Bible that is commonly, and perhaps generally, misunderstood and perverted, and supposed to teach the very opposite of what it means, that passage is in Paul's letter to the Philippians, where he says, as he is going away from the believers whom he loves, 'Work out your own salvation with fear and trembling' (Phil. ii:12). The common idea as to this text is that it means that the sinner has a share in the work of securing his own salvation. As a matter of fact, it means nothing of the sort.

"Salvation is Christ's work. It is not a work that is partly Christ's and partly the sinner's. He who begins a good work will doubtless finish it. This we are to believe, and this we are to teach. Our share in our salvation is not to our credit, but to the added credit of our Saviour. A New England boy, who was brought before the church authorities as an applicant for admission, had the right idea as to this, although he expressed it quaintly.

" 'Why do you want to join the church?' asked the pastor.

" 'Because I want to show that I am a saved sinner.'

" 'Do you feel that you are saved?'

" 'Yes, sir.'

" 'Who saved you?'

" 'It was the work of Jesus Christ and of myself.'

" 'Of yourself? What was your share in the work of your salvation?'

" 'I resisted, and Jesus Christ did the rest.'

"That boy understood the case better than one who thinks that he has a part of his own salvation to accomplish by personal endeavour."

This does not mean that we are freed from any duty in the matter. As Dr. Trumbull points out in discussing "Conversion Man's Responsibility, Not God's," conversion is our turning to God, as God is always calling us to do and seeking to enable us to do. But what we turn to and what gives us power to turn is the love and life of God working in us by the death and life of Christ. "Christ died for us." That is the great objective fact in history on which our life and confidence are built—what Josiah Royce described as the great delivering deed done from without.

But it is asked, "How could a death in history long ago and far away affect us today?" As a well known and truly devoted minister has put it, "What really saves us, saves as individuals, is not something which Jesus did nineteen hundred years ago. How can a past fact have present vital power?" Well, this minister is pastor of a church in one of our great cities which occupies a site on its most prominent avenue, worth millions of dollars. If someone were to challenge the right of his church to hold this property, what would his answer be? He would produce a past deed, a paper in evidence of a past fact, an act and transaction generations ago. If you replied, "How can an old deed, done long ago, have present validity?" he could only answer by repudiating his theology. All our title deeds are of the past. All that we have and are we owe to the past. The present is no more independent of the past than the future is of the present. In reality, time is an organic thing.

"All that is at all,
Lasts ever past recall."

And the death of Christ is the great central fact, as present in life today as it ever was and as it forever will be. For this death was a great cosmic deed. It was in time, but it is above time. The Lamb of Calvary was slain before the foundation of the world (Rev. xiii:8; I Peter i:20). Our whole salvation was there. The Kingdom which Jesus came preaching was prepared from the foundation of the world (Matt. xxv:34). The Son was loved not in His earthly mission only, but from the foundation of the world (John xvii:24). We were chosen in Christ before the foundation of the world (Eph. i:4). And what was before the world will be after. The everlasting throne is the throne of God and of the Lamb (Rev. xxii:1).

This is the ground of our hope. As that wise and sagacious man, Dr. F. F. Ellinwood, at times wrongly regarded as one who had over-rationalized Christianity, the pioneer in America in the field of comparative religion, one of our ablest teachers of philosophy and also greatest missionary leaders, wrote, with childlike faith, just before his death: "One who has seen so many years of blessings has no right to complain. The one thing which is most clear and emphatic in my consciousness is the fact that any hope I cherish must rest on foundations outside of myself. I have no complacency in the record of my life. From my present standpoint I see more clearly than ever before the absolute need of a vicarious salvation. I shall go down to the tomb resting in this alone."

"My hope is built on nothing less
Than Jesus' blood and righteousness."

And here is the ground not of all our hope alone but also of our duty. "For the love of Christ constraineth us; because we thus judge, that one died for all, therefore all died; and He died for all, that they that live should no longer live unto themselves, but unto Him who for their sakes died and rose again" (II Cor. v:14, 15).

As a simple-hearted freight brakeman on the Pennsylvania Railroad put it once long ago as we rode together in an open freight car, "He died my death for me that I might live His life for Him."

IV

WHAT THE RESURRECTION OF CHRIST MEANS TO ME

SOME years ago there appeared in Scotland a unique little volume of biography entitled *Men of the Knotted Heart*. The title was the translation of a Hebrew idiom for friendship. The book was the story of a lifelong friendship between two Scotchmen. One was a Covenanter minister named Struthers and the other a minister of the Free Church named Grant. The little book was a masterpiece of literary skill and the fragrance of the heather breathed from every page. One chapter would deal with Grant, the next with Struthers. Then the third would knot the two lives together and thus to the end. The book and the friendship were alike classic.

The two men lived for a generation in Greenock and they were as remarkable as two distinctive personalities as they were in their friendship. James Denney regarded Struthers as in some respects the most remarkable man in Scotland. He refused the degree of D.D. from Glasgow University. And it was honorary and costless! He watered his ink and reburnt his matches to save money for missions. He kept a garden and hung a basket of roses on his street gate for every passerby to help himself. He was a rock of integrity in the city and one could not tell which exceeded, his whimsical humour or his sheer intellectual genius. He loved the old landmarks, but he knew history and he believed that a living God was leading life on. He wearied of hearing Scotchmen lament the good old days that were gone, and he prepared a lecture on "The Good Old Times One Hundred Years Ago," which he would go anywhere to deliver free, in order to cure folk of their false idealization of the past.

Perhaps the most remarkable thing about Struthers was his method of playing golf. He eschewed clubs and played by hand. He could not throw as far as his competitors could drive, but he kept his direction and could stay in the fairway and out of the bunkers. His game had its orthodox rules and he held his own in the foursome in which he played with Grant and two others whose game was orthodox. On one occasion, however, both his method and the friendship came near to explosion. The players were tired on the last green. Struthers' ball lay very badly eight feet from the cup. For a long time he contemplated the situation and then the inspiration came. Walking up to his ball and planting his feet behind it, he picked it up, lay down flat on the ground and by reaching out could just drop his ball into the hole. There was a fierce demonstration over the issue. Was such an act orthodox under the system or was it heresy and crime? Struthers prevailed and the games and the friendship went on.

But all this is only incident. The story comes to the essential thing. These two men belonged to a club in Greenock to which each Monday, at least, they were accustomed to go. It was observed that Grant never entered the Club without stopping at the door with his hand on the knob and whispering something softly to himself. It came to be a matter of curious comment, and someone spoke to Struthers about it. "Have you noticed," he asked, "that whenever Grant comes in he stops at the door and speaks to himself? I wonder what it is that he says! Do you know?" "Why, yes," Struthers replied, "I know. He says 'Christ is risen.' " That was his way of keeping the central fact of Christian faith and experience in its central place in his life, of holding his life in common things and in daily incidents under the basic fact and the supreme principle of Christianity, the Resurrection of Christ.

There were few, if indeed there were any, of the delegates to the International Missionary Council in Jerusalem in 1928, to whom that Holy Week and Easter Day did not bring a new sense of the place of the Resurrection in Christian faith and its meaning in Christian experience. On Maundy Thursday evening we had all gone to the little Anglican Church of St. George, by the Jaffa Gate, near the great breach in the wall through which Allenby and his army came in when they entered Jerusalem in the World War. There we sat down together in the Communion Supper of our Lord, men and women of all lands and races and branches of the one Church of Christ. After the Supper we passed out in a long company through the deserted streets of the city, through David Street past the silent bazaars to the Via Dolorosa, past the Church of the Holy Sepulchre and the Church of St. Anne over the pavement of Herod's Judgment Hall, past the Pool of Bethesda and out through St. Stephen's Gate and across the Brook Kidron to the slope of Olivet and the Garden of Gethsemane. There we sat down together under the old gnarled olive trees to keep such watch together as those sleepy and weary disciples failed to keep, while the rain clouds scudded across the sky and we prayed together in many tongues but with one heart, and cuddled close together to keep off the chill wind. In thought and memory we followed Jesus that night as He was harried from court to court, and the next day we walked with the great company of the pilgrims from many lands by all the Seven Stations of the Cross and lived through, as well as love and imagination could, the Supreme Tragedy, until they had laid Him in His grave. So it was all over.

> "Now He is dead, far hence He lies
> In that lone Syrian town,
> And on His grave with shining eyes
> The silent stars look down."

All the pathos and disappointment of those first disciples we could in a measure feel. "We trusted," the two disciples said, "we trusted that it had been He which should have redeemed Israel." And now all that was past.

What a day that Saturday between Good Friday and Easter must have been. Here is work for the Christian imagination—to go back and live through that interval with the first disciples. I have a good friend, a judge in the District Courts of the Federal Government, who is accustomed each year to shut himself in his library during this last day of Holy Week and to try to go back into that Saturday in Jerusalem and to think and feel what the disciples must have thought and felt. And then after that, and the doubt and darkness of it, comes the jubilant dawn of the Easter Sabbath. What it must have been to that little company we can feel in the glorious and tingling joy of Peter's long-after reminiscence: "Blessed be the God and Father of our Lord Jesus Christ, who according to His great mercy begat us again unto a living hope by the Resurrection of Jesus

Christ from the dead." We felt just that in Jerusalem on our Easter Day at the great Conference. We had gone early in the morning, some to the so-called "Tomb in the Garden" near Gordon's Calvary and some to the ancient "Tomb of the Kings" with the great stone rolled from the grave just as it must have been that far-off day. There we had read the story of the first Easter and then made our way up the Mount of Olives to the German Hospice and were sitting together in memory and expectation of Christ in the meeting hall. As we sat, it seemed that any moment the door might have flown open and Peter and John burst in with their amazing news: "He is risen. We have been at the tomb. The door is open. He is not there. The garments that wrapped Him are lying in the chrysalis that contained Him, but He is risen. He may be here at any moment. Anything can happen now with Jesus back, conqueror of death."

This was what the Resurrection was and is—new life. "Stanley," said David Livingstone in his loneliness, with all his resources exhausted and his work nearly done, as Stanley brought him news of the whole world's thought of him and equipped him again for what he wished still to do, "Stanley, you have brought me new life. You have brought me new life." In a measure infinitely transcending this the Resurrection was as life from the dead to the men who had found in Christ their Heavenly Lord and then had seemed to lose Him on the Cross.

They had now, as we also have in the Resurrection, a clear and irrefutable assurance of faith. It is significant to note that from the first they realized this. Simon Peter, who in the High Priest's palace had been intimidated by the taunts of a servant maid, is now afraid of no one and draws his new confidence and courage from the Resurrection (Acts ii:22-36; iii:11-16; iv:5-12). And this was the inpregnable basis of Paul's faith. He begins his letter to the Romans with a statement of the ground of His belief in the deity of Christ. What was that ground? Not the character of Christ, nor His teaching, nor the unity and harmony of His personality such as Paul had longed for and not been able to achieve for himself, nor His unique and central place in history, nor His mighty works. None of these. "He was declared to be the Son of God with power," says Paul, "by His Resurrection from the dead." And so we also who have known the Risen Christ are assured beyond all doubt.

And the Resurrection was to the primitive Christian company, and it is to us, the principle of a new life. "We were buried therefore with Him through baptism into death: that like as Christ was raised from the dead through the glory of the Father, so we also might walk in newness of life. For if we have become united with Him in the likeness of His death, we shall be also in the likeness of His Resurrection" (Rom. vi:4, 5). "Wherefore if any man is in Christ, he is a new creature: the old things are passed away; behold, they are become new" (II Cor. v:17). "If then ye were raised together with Christ, seek the things that are above, where Christ is, seated on the right hand of God. Set your mind on the things that are above, not on the things that are upon the earth. For ye died, and your life is hid with Christ in God" (Col. iii:1-3).

Some years ago I spent the Easter season with friends among the Moravians in Bethlehem, Pennsylvania. Beginning on Wednesday we met together in the lovely old church and read the connected story of the last days of Jesus' life, the readings interspersed with the glorious Bach music. All the shadows of the Crucifixion came upon us as we watched our Saviour die upon His Cross. But the Easter Dawn was to come, and early that Lord's Day morning while it was yet dark we were wakened by the trombones from the Church belfry and by the sound of the hurrying footsteps on the streets. When we came with the others into the church we found it filled with the folk sitting in the expectant silence—broken when the ministers in white came through the door before us and the senior minister paused in the doorway and cried to us, "Christ is risen," and we answered him back, "Yea, Christ is risen." Then we all passed out into the old cemetery beside the church and standing in a great cross between the four quarters of the graveyard we sang the great Easter hymns until the sun came up over the eastern hills beyond the river. I recall the experience because behind us in the quarter of the cemetery where the little boys were buried, the men, women and little girls having each their quarter too, we noted a simple stone bearing this inscription:

> "How does our Saviour look?
> 'Right clean,' was his reply."

No one knows the history of this stone or the authentic meaning of its inscription. Was the little lad so near the Land Beyond that through the fading veil he seemed to see the Risen Lord, and did someone ask him what he saw and get the answer: "One Right Clean?" It might have been so, for clean is the Resurrection Life and those who rise with Christ, whatever their outer garments, are called to walk by the principle of a new and clean life, "whiter than snow."

And this is not a vain call, nor a call to try to do for ourselves what by ourselves we can never do. The fact of the Resurrection is the evidence of the availability of power, "the exceeding greatness," as Paul says, "of God's power to usward who believe, according to that working of the strength of His might which He wrought in Christ when He raised Him from the dead," a gift for which Paul counted everything else as dross, that as he said, "I may gain Christ, and be found in Him, not having a righteousness of mine own, even that which is of the law, but that which is through faith in Christ, the righteousness which is from God by faith: that I may know Him, and the power of His Resurrection, and the fellowship of His sufferings, becoming conformed unto His death; if by any means I may attain unto the Resurrection from the dead" (Phil. iii:9-11). And this power has been given and is available for every man—power adequate for every human need. A Saviour who conquered death can conquer anything. A Saviour who redeemed mankind can achieve anything.

The Resurrection is not only a new experience, principle and form of life; it was and is a new message. It was the message of primitive Christianity. Harnack judges that the four great notes in the early preaching of Christianity across the ancient world were God the Father and Creator, Jesus the Saviour and Redeemer, purity and the Resurrection. The Resurrection was the centre of thought for early Christianity. Two little touches in Paul's letters reveal its place. In the passage just quoted from Philippians note the order, not first the sufferings of Christ and then the Resurrection, but the reverse. And in his second letter to Timothy there is an even more striking instance. The King

James' version of II Timothy ii:8 reads: "Remember that Jesus Christ of the seed of David was raised from the dead according to my gospel." But note the reading in the American Standard Revised: "Remember Jesus Christ, risen from the dead, of the seed of David, according to my gospel." "Risen from the dead" is the first thing. "Of the seed of David" is secondary. And this was deliberate with Paul. There was no doubt whatever in his mind as to what the central thing in Christianity is, and he stated his conviction in a way that utterly dislocates many theological systems, and denies the adequacy of the death of Christ save as that death was followed and complemented by the Resurrection. "And if Christ hath not been raised, then is our preaching vain, your faith also is vain. Yea, and we are found false witnesses of God; because we witnessed of God that He raised up Christ: whom He raised not up, if so be that the dead are not raised. For if the dead are not raised, neither hath Christ been raised; and if Christ hath not been raised, your faith is vain; ye are yet in your sins" (I Cor. xv:14-17).

This Resurrection was the great topic in the first Christian preaching. It was required in the choice of a successor to Judas that he could be a witness to the Resurrection. It was the central and essential note in the sermons that are preserved, Peter's sermon on Pentecost (Acts ii:32, cf. Acts iv:33), and in the house of Cornelius (Acts x:40, 41), Paul's sermon at Antioch of Pisidia (Acts xiii:34), and at Athens on Mars Hill (Acts xvii:18, 31, 32). To the Corinthians Paul wrote that the gospel which he preached was the message of the Resurrection and that if the Resurrection were not true then his preaching was vain, the Christian faith was vain and there was no salvation of men from their sins.

What the Resurrection was in the life and thought alike of the early Christians it is in ours. It must be the centre of our thought and of our message. This is the Gospel of joy. The Cross alone is stark tragedy. Add the Resurrection, and the Cross is luminous with glory and victory.

The companionship of the first Christians and our companionship is with the Risen and Living Christ. Before He died He made a great promise to His disciples. "Nevertheless I tell you the truth: It is expedient for you that I go away; for if I go not away, the Comforter will not come unto you; but if I go, I will send Him unto you" (John xvi:7). And not the Comforter only, but He Himself was to be with them. "And ye therefore now have sorrow: but I will see you again, and your heart shall rejoice, and your joy no one taketh away from you." And they did see Him again and had His renewed promise, "Lo, I am with you always, even unto the end of the world." Here was no condition. He did not say as with so many other promises, "If you will, I will," but He states a fact that is to be, regardless of aught else. Christ is with us. There is no more objective fact of human history, nor any more indisputably true, than this of the presence of Christ in the life of the world and in the lives of men. Death removed Him from a local fellowship that He might be through the Resurrection the companion of men everywhere and always, in every land and in every age. Thousands upon thousands can testify that He is our inseparable companion, and that we are accompanied with Him and in Him by those whom we love and have lost from our earthly sight and touch, but who are near, members of that encompassing host of whom the Epistle to the Hebrews speaks (Heb. xii:1). I do not believe that there is communication in human speech between us and them. Some time ago a friend sent me a series of messages which some woman in New Hampshire claimed to have received from Phillips Brooks, but either they were unauthentic or Phillips Brooks had undergone a pitiful intellectual and spiritual deterioration, had forgotten both the spelling and grammar of the language of which he was such a master on earth, and the glorious visions of truth given him here had faded for him in the life beyond. William James used to say that if it was possible for the spirits of the departed to speak to us who remain he would assuredly send us word, but it is evident that even his ingenious and untiring spirit has found no way. But the dead live, by the witness of the Resurrection, and they live with us because Christ lives with us and they are in Christ, and we may speak to them in Him as we speak to Him. They are busy, we are sure, in the affairs of Him Who was dead but is alive again and lo, He is alive forevermore.

The Resurrection of Christ is the guarantee of the possibility of radical moral and spiritual breach. The principle of discontinuity is as real and authentic as the principle of continuity. No adequate evidence has been found in support of an absolute principle of continuity even in nature. Still less can it be found in the nature of the will and the soul. New habits can be formed, as James held, until the last day of life and old habits can be broken up to the last day. It is the principle of discontinuity with which every surgeon does his work and so also every surgeon of the soul.

Some years ago after a Sunday at Yale I received the following letter:

"I want to tell you of the result of your talk at Dwight Hall tonight. Though I have been a professing Christian and a member of the ——— Church I have not been conquering sin in my life in one respect. The way you put it tonight someway helped me to believe that Christ could give me victory and I do believe and count on Him. This has been the battle ground in my thought. Can Christ actually overcome the circumstances and the ordinary course of consequences in a man's life without waiting for the slow natural processes of habit breaking and habit formation? I now know that he can—that he can enable a man to right about face in an instant. If he cannot there is no excuse for Christianity. The particular point which helped me I think was the idea that Christ could help a man get the bulge on his temptation *at the first,* and that he could thus *actually become a different man.*

"I wish to thank you for your message. I am a graduate student in psychology and I think the desire to explain everything by psychological laws has been a stumbling block to me. The change in men's lives is just as hard and solid a fact as any other, and if our philosophy won't assimilate it, so much the worse for our philosophy. The fact remains a blessing for the man who realizes it. And I am thankful I am one who does."

The Resurrection of Christ was in one sense an illustration of the highest form of the law of continuity. As Godet says: "It is said: Such a fact would overthrow the laws of nature. But what if it were, on the contrary, the law of nature, when thoroughly understood, which required this fact? Death is the wages of sin. If Jesus lived here below as innocent and pure, if He lived in God and of God, as He Himself says in John vi:57, life must be the crown of this unique conqueror. No doubt He may have given Himself up voluntarily to death to fulfil the law which condemn sinful humanity; but might not this state of death affecting a nature perfectly sound, morally and phys ically, meet in it exceptional forces capable of reactin victoriously against all the powers of dissolution? A necessarily as a life of sin ends in death, so necessaril does perfect holiness end in life, and consequently (i there has been death) in the Resurrection."

Paul's word is confirmation of this view. "Jesu Christ," he says, in words already partially quoted "was declared to be the Son of God with power, *accord ing to the spirit of holiness*, by His Resurrection fron the dead" (Rom. i:4). The Resurrection as evidenc of the law of absolute moral purity is witness to th integrity of the divine order. Jesus Christ, as we hav seen, could not be holden of death. It was not pos sible in the universe of such a God as the righteous an loving God and Father of Jesus Christ.

But the Resurrection viewed from the side of ou morally disordered world was a proof of the principl of discontinuity. He broke the bars of death. H came back from the grave, and the breach that H made in the regularity of our human moral disabilit and the continuing grip of sin, is valid and availabl for all of us. "For if we have become united with Hin in the likeness of His death, we shall be also in th likeness of His Resurrection; knowing this, that our ol man was crucified with Him, that the body of si might be done away, that so we should no longer be i bondage to sin: for He that hath died is justified fron sin. But if we died with Christ, we believe that w shall also live with Him; knowing that Christ bein raised from the dead dieth no more; death no mor hath dominion over Him. For the death that He died,

He died unto sin once: but the life that He liveth, He liveth unto God. Even so reckon ye also, yourselves to be dead unto sin, but alive unto God in Christ Jesus. Let not sin therefore reign in your mortal body, that ye should obey the lusts thereof: neither present your members unto sin as instruments of unrighteousness; but present yourselves unto God, as alive from the dead, and your members as instruments of righteousness unto God. For sin shall not have dominion over you: for ye are not under law, but under grace" (Rom. vi:5-14).

Lastly the Resurrection is the supreme proof of the possibility of achieving victory not over defeat but by and through defeat. There are two terrifically bold declarations in the New Testament. One is in the letter to the Corinthians, "Him Who knew no sin He made to be sin on our behalf that we might become the righteousness of God in Him." The other is in the letter to the Hebrews: "Since then the children are sharers in flesh and blood, He also Himself in like manner partook of the same; that through death He might bring to nought him that had the power of death, that is, the devil; and might deliver all them who through fear of death were all their lifetime subject to bondage."

In other words, Christ took sin and death to stop sin and death. The truth here is bottomless. No human words or system of thought can compass this fulness and mystery. But the principle is clear as light. He conquered death by death and sin by sin—He Who was Life and Who knew no sin. Can honour and glory and power go further than this?

A little, so very little, and yet something of the reality of such a law of victory by and through defeat, is in Howard Pyle's story, *Men of Iron,* a glorious boys' story of a training school for young knights in the fifteenth century. Lord Falworth had been deprived of his estates and attainted through the influence of his enemy, the Earl of Alban, who would have had the old blind lord killed if he had known where he could be found. The only hope of any escape or restoration lay in the possibility of a victory in single combat between Myles Falworth, the old lord's only son, and the all powerful Earl who had the ear of the King. For this combat Sir James Lee trained the boy, and the picture of the training school is a noble thing. At last the boy's day came and before the King and the Court he fought for his father's honour and his father's life. Three times in the foolishness of his chivalry Myles spared his foe, and then in an unguarded moment his unprincipled enemy got the advantage and used it dishonourably as the lad lay imprisoned in his armour on the ground. After that this is the story:

"For the third time the Earl swung the blade flashing, and then it fell, straight and true, upon the defenceless body, just below the left arm, biting deep through the armour plates. For an instant the blade stuck fast, and that instant was Myles's salvation. Under the agony of the blow he gave a muffled cry, and almost instinctively grasped the shaft of the weapon with both hands. Had the Earl let go his end of the weapon, he would have won the battle at his leisure and most easily; as it was, he struggled violently to wrench the gisarm away from Myles. In that short, fierce struggle Myles was dragged to his knees, and then, still holding the weapon with one hand, he clutched the trappings of the Earl's horse with the other. The next moment he was upon his feet. The other struggled to thrust him away, but Myles, letting go the gisarm, which he held with his left hand, clutched him tightly by the sword-belt in the intense, vise-like grip of despair. In vain the Earl strove to beat him loose with the shaft of the gisarm, in vain he spurred and reared his horse to shake him off; Myles held him tight, in spite of all his struggles.

"He felt neither the streaming blood nor the throbbing agony of his wounds; every faculty of soul, mind, body, every power of life, was centred in one intense, burning effort. He neither felt, thought, nor reasoned, but clutching, with the blindness of instinct, the heavy, spiked, iron-headed mace that hung at the Earl's saddle-bow, he gave it one tremendous wrench that snapped the plaited leathern thongs that held it as though they were skeins of thread. Then, grinding his teeth as with a spasm, he struck as he had never struck before—once, twice, thrice full upon the front of the helmet. Crash! crash! And then, even as the Earl toppled sidelong, crash! And the iron plates split and crackled under the third blow. Myles had one flashing glimpse of an awful face, and then the saddle was empty." [1]

So that was his defeat and his victory, victory won out of and by defeat.

It is a feeble illustration, as all human illustrations must be. But this was the glory of Christ's Cross and Resurrection. By death he slew death. The Cross conquered Him and by the Cross He conquered sin and hell. After Him follows the company of the redeemed.

---

[1] Howard Pyle, *Men of Iron* (Harpers).

V

WHAT THE LORDSHIP OF CHRIST MEANS TO ME

MODERN literature has found its favourite title for Jesus in the word "Master." It is found in the title of many books about Jesus: *Christ and Other Masters, The Mind of the Master, The Manhood of the Master, The Life of the Master, The Master of the Heart, The Steps of the Master,* and probably scores more. Sometimes, though by no means always, the word is used in a naturalistic interest, to bring Jesus wholly within our human categories. It does not need to be said that such a use is widely at variance with the thought of the New Testament, and it is that thought and the response to it in our own experience that we are to consider now.

There is no title of Jesus more frequently used in its various forms in the New Testament than this. And the poverty of our English speech when compared with the Greek is seen in the fact that there are five different Greek words all translated by our one English word "Master," and that some of these words have to be otherwise translated elsewhere because they are of a wider meaning even than "master." We shall need to study these words one by one to get the full New Testament meaning of Christ's Lordship. Let us take them in the order of the measure of their significance.

The first is the simple Greek word for "teacher," *didaskalos,* or its Hebrew equivalent "Rabbi." It is used at the beginning of Jesus' ministry. The Revised Version translates it here "Teacher," and the King James, "Master:" "Then Jesus turned, and saw them following, and saith unto them, What seek ye? They said unto Him, Rabbi, (which is to say, being interpreted, Master,) where dwellest Thou?" (John i:38, King James Version). And it is used at the end, where the two versions translate as before "Teacher" and "Master:" "Jesus saith unto her, Mary. She turned herself, and saith unto Him, Rabboni; which is to say, Master" (John xx:16, King James Version). More than forty times the word *didaskalos* or teacher is translated "Master" in our old version. In every case the American Standard Revised translates the word, "Teacher." This then is first. The acceptance of the Lordship or Mastery of Jesus means for a man his recognition of Jesus as his teacher.

The whole world is agreed in its admiration of the skill and power of Jesus as a teacher. The testimony of the Temple police sent to arrest Him is the general testimony, "Never man spake like this Man." He was pre-eminently a teacher. This is one of our first glimpses of Him (Matt. iv:23). Luke summarizes His ministry as a work of doing and teaching (Acts i:1). On this faculty He Himself laid emphasis (Matt. xiii:52; xxviii:19, 20).

There was need among His own disciples for such teaching (Matt. xv:15, 16; John xiv:8, 9; Luke xxiv:25, 26). His work was continual discussion (John vi; vii; viii). Notice how, in these chapters, Jesus leads on the open-minded to full faith, and sets before those of hostile, fleshly heart the plain fact, put in innumerable ways, that spiritual truth requires a spiritual vision.

Jesus succeeded by teaching in the simplest and most human ways. He sought to combine the greatest clearness with the briefest compass, avoiding always "all considerations and circumstances which, though neither multiplying nor limiting the general principles to be taught, would in any degree obscure them."[1] He teaches thus by example, as, "after giving the exhortation not to resist one that is evil, He subjoins the example of how to act if struck by another on the right cheek, or if robbed by him of a coat through form of legal process" (Matt. i:39-41). He teaches also by object lessons (John xiii:1-20), and as frequently by comparisons, illustrative similes (Mark x:15; Matt. x:16; xiii:27; Luke xiii:34), or similes extended into parables (Mark iv:33, 34); recognizing the truth that

> "Truth in closest words shall fail
> When truth embodied in a tale
> Shall enter in at lowly doors;
>
> "Which they may read who bind the sheaf
> Or build the house or dig the grave,
> Or those wild eyes which watch the wave
> In roarings round the coral reef."

His teaching was constantly from the things He saw, signs of the high realities (Matt. vi:28). What suggested the figures in Matthew v:14; John iii:8; iv:10, 34, 35; vi:35; vii: 37, 38; viii:12; xv:17? Sometimes this symbolic teaching was direct and intentional (Mark ix:33-37), and sometimes indirect (Mark viii:14-21). As in this last case, He asked questions constantly (Matt. xiii:51; xvii:24-27; xxii:15-22); or, as in John iv and vi, constantly hinted more than

[1] H. Wendt, *The Teaching of Jesus,* Vol. I, p. 131 (Scribners).

His auditors were able at the time to apprehend, and so led them on toward the large truth which lay beyond His hints.

He constantly and unweariedly taught, not afraid of wasting time or truth on barren souls. Meeting a poor woman by a well-side, He at once begins a conversation, and leads her on from truth to truth, till the larger light breaks over her (John iv:1-26). All interruptions He uses for the purposes of His teaching. They never disconcert Him (John xiii:25, 36; xiv:5, 8, 22). Even on social occasions He turned the conversation to the deeper themes (Luke xi:37-40), but He did it always in a perfectly genuine and natural way. He could do this (1) because of the vigour of His spiritual perceptions. He saw truth ever, and the things of which He spoke were wholly real to Him (John v:19, 20). He did not speculate, or speak perfunctorily, as one whose profession it was to preach. To lead men into light was His life. (2) His teaching was self-revelation. He was the truth He taught. To speak was to teach the eternal vitalities (John viii:12; xiv:6).

His followers were properly called "disciples," learners. And it is no wonder that Nicodemus declared, voicing what was evidently, at the time, the conviction of his class, "We know that Thou art a teacher come from God." "Teacher" was His popular title, and today even those who do not accede to the claim of His supreme divinity look up to Him as the great Teacher, "that unexampled Rabbi."

As a teacher, He combined constructive strength with the most complete mastery of the destructive processes of the Socratic method. Nowhere is this more beautifully shown than in the sixth chapter of the Gospel of John, where, in verses 26–40, a dialogue with the people, He lays bare the mercenary character of their discipleship, and mercilessly attacks the search for "fodder," upon which, like beasts, they have set out, and concludes with the direct and unmistakable assertion of truths, which He frankly tells them they would not understand because they were unwilling to meet the conditions of understanding. In verses 41–51, in an open answer to secret murmuring of the Jews, He offers His secret with sublime tact to any man who has the spiritual illumination to respond to Him, taking thus the best road to the heart of any open-minded man present, throwing Himself on that man's candour and courage; and in verses 52–59 He clinches His appeal to such a man by yet more open and bold assertion, at the risk of alienating yet more the many who had no capacity to respond.

But the wonder of Jesus' direct teaching was equalled by the wonder of His teaching by influence, by personal presence. One of the most notable illustrations of this is the story of the woman taken in adultery whom a group of Scribes and Pharisees caught in the act and brought to Jesus. Where was the man? They must have caught him, too. Why did they not bring him also to Jesus? One can feel in the story the salacious pride of the group as they dragged the poor creature with them before Jesus. And Jesus answered them never a word. Perhaps it was indignation, perhaps it was shame at the degradation of the humanity He had come to save. He stooped over in silence and wrote with His fingers in the sand. What did He write? "Scribes, Pharisees, hypocrites?" Then He rose and spake once and lo, in Christ's presence and at His word, it all took on a totally different aspect. What had seemed to them a glorious outburst of moral honour began to look tawdry and contemptible and *beginning at the oldest* they slunk out, leaving the woman alone with Jesus. This is the effect of atmosphere. In O. Henry's story the tempted shop girl grew strong again as she looked at the clean face of Kitchener on the mantle in her poor hall bedroom. John Watson told once of a man who kept a jar of faded rose leaves on his office table and when he needed courage and strength and moral steadfastness, the man would take up a handful of the leaves and their fragrance carried him back to his boyhood home and the library window opening out on the rose bushes on the lawn, and the breath of that home's honour would come back and he would decide and do as in the presence of the purity and truth of the old father who had dwelt there. "In Thy light shall we see light."

And Jesus Christ taught what no one else knew—about God and man and duty and life. And He was the lesson He taught. Men learned Him (Eph. iv:20; Matt. xi:29). And all that He was as the Master Who was a teacher, He is to us who call Him Master today. We live in His school and we learn of Him and we learn Him.

The second word in our Greek Testament which is translated "Master," in both the King James and the Revised Version, is *kathegetes*. It occurs in but one passage, Matt. xxiii:8-10: "Neither be ye called masters, for one is your Master even Christ." The word means literally "Leader." And there is no word whose meaning we better know. Every boy knows the game of "Follow the leader." In every sphere of life some men lead and others follow. And the supreme leadership was authoritatively assumed and claimed by Christ. His first and last summons was "Follow Me." "And walking by the sea of Galilee, He saw two brethren, Simon who is called Peter, and Andrew his brother, casting a net into the sea; for they were fishers. And He saith unto them, come ye after Me, and I will make you fishers of men. And they straightway left the nets, and followed Him" (Matt. iv:18-20). This was at the beginning. His summons was the same at the end when by the Sea of Galilee Peter asked Him about the destiny of John: "Jesus saith unto him, if I will that he tarry till I come, what is that to thee? Follow thou Me" (John xxi:22). And continuously throughout His ministry this was His call to men. "Then said Jesus unto His disciples, if any man would come after Me, let him deny himself, and take up his cross, and follow Me" (Matt. xvi:24). "Jesus said unto him, if thou wouldest be perfect, go, sell that which thou hast, and give to the poor, and thou shalt have treasure in heaven: and come, follow Me" (Matt. xix:21). "If any man serve Me, let him follow Me; and where I am, there shall also My servant be: if any man serve Me, him will the Father honour" (John xii:26).

To both Paul and Peter, following God in Christ was the essence of Christian discipleship. "Be ye therefore imitators of God, as beloved children; and walk in love, even as Christ also loved you, and gave Himself up for us, an offering and a sacrifice to God for an odour of a sweet smell" (Eph. v:1). "For hereunto were ye called: because Christ also suffered for you, leaving you an example, that ye should follow His steps" (I Peter ii:21). And the host which John saw in his vision, in whose mouth was found no lie and who were without blemish, were "they that follow the Lamb whithersoever He goeth."

And this is the note of our Christian hymns which preserve both our sound theology and our true experience:

"He leadeth me, O blessed thought."
"Lead on, O King Eternal."
"Saviour, like a shepherd lead us."
"By pastures green He leadeth me."
"Where He leads me, I will follow."
"Jesus, Saviour, pilot me."
"Who follows in His train?"

To the early Christian conscience and to us, Jesus, the Lord and Master, is leader, example, ideal, such as every man needs and must find somewhere. "I feel lost now," said a college undergraduate to a friend. "George was an ideal for me. He was for me in the place of God, and now that he has died I don't know what to do." And all the time the perfect Leader from whom George had learned whatever he knew was at hand and waiting.

The world today is lost for lack of the acceptance of the leadership of Jesus Christ as Lord. He would never lead it into war, or hatred, or selfishness, or wrong, or suffering that springs from sin. It is a false comfort that is often offered to us in some great sorrow to be assured that God's will is best and that we must see in our sorrow His greater wisdom and love. There is no doubt a wise and loving chastening, but it is blasphemy to charge God with complicity in murder or lust or sin. God cannot be tempted by evil, nor tempteth any man. And there is no iniquity in Him. All that is evil and wrong is in deadly opposition to His will, which is "good and acceptable and perfect."

Where will the Lordship of Jesus lead us if we will follow it? Into peace (Rom. xiv:19; Heb. xii:14). Into love (I Cor. xiv:1). Into all good (I Thess. v:15). Into righteousness (I Tim. vi:11). Into the company of all faithful souls who build together with God (I Thess. ii:14; Heb. vi:12; I Cor. iii:9; II Cor. v:19-21; vi:1).

This is no call to weaklings nor to a timid and futile venture. The men to whom it first came had to burn their bridges behind them and move out on an adventure in comparison with which the worst storms and perils of their fishing life on Galilee were child's play. They set out, only gradually realizing their mission as they went on, to supplant the religious institutions of their race, to upheave the Roman Empire, to establish a new order on the earth and to pay for their undertaking with their lives. In this, as in all else, they followed their Leader. The Lordship of Christ means no less for us today.

"If I find Him, if I follow,
What His guerdon here?
Many a sorrow, many a labour,
Many a tear.

"If I still hold closely to Him,
What hath He at last?
'Sorrow vanquished, labour ended,
Jordan passed.' "

"Finding, following, keeping, struggling,
Is He sure to bless?
'Saints, apostles, prophets, martyrs,
Answer, Yes.' "

The third of these New Testament words for "Master" is found only in the Gospel according to Luke, and there it occurs six times (Luke v:5; viii:24, 45; ix:33, 49; xvii:13). And not elsewhere in the Bible. It was the word used by Peter in reply to Jesus' counsel after the fruitless night of fishing, "Master, we toiled all night and took nothing: but at Thy word I will let down the nets." It was the cry of the disciples in the storm, "Master, Master, we perish." It was Peter's word on the Mount of Transfiguration, "Master, it is good for us to be here;" and John's shortly after, "Master, we saw one casting out demons in Thy name and we forbade him." And it was the word of appeal from the ten lepers, "Jesus, Master, have mercy on us." Luke uses two of the other words translated "Master," but on these occasions he chose this one, even though other evangelists in reporting some of the same incidents use wholly different words. Why did Luke choose this one? Well, its pertinence is obvious. It is the word *epistates*, and it means literally "superintendent" or "overseer." That was just what Jesus was on these occasions. And that is what His Mastery or Lordship involves always, in the days of His flesh and today.

He gives us our work. One of Horace Bushnell's greatest sermons, condensed, with his characteristic genius, into the title, is "Every Man's Life a Plan of God." "To every man his work" was the way our Lord expressed it. "It is as when a man, sojourning in another country, having left his house, and given authority to his servants, to each one his work, commanded also the porter to watch. Watch therefore: for ye know not when the lord of the house cometh, whether at even, or at midnight, or at cockcrowing, or in the morning; lest coming suddenly he find you sleeping. And what I say unto you I say unto all,

Watch" (Mark xiii:34-37). In many parables Jesus set forth this relation between Him and His disciples. In each of them He gives a trust to keep and fulfil—talents, pounds, powers. We are not sent into the world adrift. We may indeed refuse to be guided, but we came each with a personal, divine assignment which has been always seeking us more zealously than we have sought it. The work of His appointing is our true work and will make its own accounting.

> "My new cut ashlar takes the light
> Where crimson blank the windows flare
> By my own work before the night,
> Great Overseer, I make my prayer."

And the Lord and Master Who is the Superintendent gives us both our work and such a passion for it as He had for His! The zeal of His Father's business consumed Him (John ii:17). He had no leisure so much as to eat (Mark vi:31). So busy was He that His own friends said He was beside Himself (Mark iii:21). And He summoned His disciples to share His work with Him. "We must work," He said to them, "the works of Him that sent Me, while it is day: the night cometh when no man can work" (John ix:4). Those words, "The night cometh," are painted in Greek over the fireplace of the library in Rudyard Kipling's old home in Brattleboro, Vermont. Stanley was asked once which of all his lieutenants in Africa had been most satisfactory and he answered, "Glave. He was one of those men who relish a task for its bigness and greet hard labour with a fierce joy." And many years ago the late Professor Brackett, one of the greatest physicists of his day and a pioneer in the field of electrical engineering, told a group of students, in witnessing to His Christian faith, that when a student himself he had had a friend who later went as a foreign missionary, with whom in their college days he had prayed this prayer, "O Lord, we pledge ourselves to live with a vengeance and to die with a snap." The dying at the end of such a life can safely be left in the hands of the Overseer, Who is Lord of Life and of Death, and Who will do what is best for His workmen, but Who cannot be displeased with the prayer:

> "I ask no heaven till earth be Thine
> No glory crown while work of mine
> Remaineth here.
> When earth shall shine among the stars,
> Her sins cast out, her captives free,
> Her voice a music unto Thee,
> For crown?
> More work give Thou to me.
> Lord, here I am."

The fourth word for "Master" is one of the most common words in the New Testament, the word *kurios*. It may be only a term of human address like "Sir," as in John xii:21, "Sir, we would see Jesus," or a word for a human sovereign as in Acts xxv:26, or it may mean "owner," the opposite of slave, and with reference to Jesus it is used and translated as both "Master" and "Lord." It appears in the sense of Lord hundreds of times in the New Testament. Indeed with half a dozen exceptions it is the only word translated Lord, and with only a few exceptions it is invariably so translated. Jesus used the word in the sense of "master" in Matthew vi:24, Mark xiii:35, Luke xiv:21 and xvi:13, and Paul, who uses the word hundreds of times when it is translated "Lord," uses it twice when it is translated both in the King James and in the American Standard Revised as "Master." "And, ye masters, do the same things unto them, and forbear threatening: knowing that He Who is both their Master and yours is in heaven, and there is no respect of persons with Him" (Eph. vi:9). "Masters, render unto your servants that which is just and equal; knowing that ye also have a Master in heaven" (Col. iv:1).

It was as his Lord and Master in the sense of absolute "owner" that Paul conceived Jesus. He called himself the *"doulos,"* the bond slave of Christ (Rom. i:1; Titus i:1; Phil. i:1). So also did James (Jas. i:1), and Peter (II Peter i:1), and Jude (Jude i), and John (Rev. i:1). And the primitive conception of discipleship was precisely this relationship. Christians belong to Christ (I Cor. iii:23; Eph. vi:6). Dr. A. J. Gordon used to say that he loved nothing more than to hear a young man call Jesus "Lord." He knew that such an one had found life's true relationships (and that is life, namely, the adjustment of the organism to its right environment),—that he had come to know the reality of things. "This is life eternal, that they should know Thee the only true God, and Him Whom Thou didst send, even Jesus Christ."

The Lord and Master, Jesus Christ, is owner of our lives. We are not our own. We belong to Him. Our business is to be our calling, the thing He calls us to. All that we are and have are to be administered as a trust from Him. The centre of our life is to be changed. We are to do our living not unto ourselves but unto Him "Who died for all, that they that live should no longer live unto themselves, but unto Him Who for their sakes died and rose again" (II Cor. v:15).

This is no servile principle. It is not the depression and dishonouring of life. The real degradation is the futile boastfulness of W. E. Henley's too familiar lines:

> "Out of the night that covers me,
> Black as the pit from pole to pole,
> I thank whatever gods may be,
> For my unconquerable soul.
>
> "In the fell clutch of circumstance
> I have not winced nor cried aloud.
> Under the bludgeonings of chance
> My head is bloody but unbowed.
>
> "Beyond this place of wrath and tears
> Looms but the Horror of the shade,
> And yet the menace of the years
> Finds and shall find me unafraid.
>
> "It matters not how strait the gate,
> How charged with punishment the scroll,
> I am the master of my fate,
> I am the captain of my soul." [2]

The acknowledgment of Christ's ownership and mastery is the unfolding, empowering and fulfilment of life.

> "I've found a Friend; O such a Friend!
> He loved me ere I knew Him;
> He drew me with the cords of love,
> And thus He bound me to Him;
> And 'round my heart still closely twine
> Those ties which naught can sever,
> For I am His and He is mine,
> For ever and for ever.

[2] W. E. Henley, *Poems* (Macmillan).

"I've found a Friend; O such a Friend!
He bled, He died to save me;
And not alone the gift of love,
But His own self He gave me.
Naught that I have mine own I'll call,
I'll hold it for the Giver;
My heart, my strength, my life, my all,
Are His, and His for ever.

"I've found a Friend; O such a Friend!
All power to Him is given,
To guard me on my onward course,
And bring me safe to heaven:
Eternal glory gleams afar,
To nerve my faint endeavour:
So now to watch, to work, to war;
And then to rest for ever.

"I've found a Friend; O such a Friend,
So kind and true and tender!
So wise a Counsellor and Guide,
So mighty a Defender!
From Him, who loves me now so well,
What power my soul can sever?
Shall life or death, shall earth or hell?
No: I am His for ever."

This recognition of Christ's ownership penetrates the whole area of life and transfers it to a different plane. A half century ago one of the heroes of the English-speaking student world was a young Scotchman named Ion Keith-Falconer. He came from one of the oldest families of Scotland whose blood had been spilt on every battle ground in Scottish history. They had been the Earls of Kintore and when that title was abolished, the Lords Marischal of Scotland. Marischal College at Aberdeen bore their family motto, "They say. What do they say? Let them say." As a boy he mastered Hebrew so as to carry on a schoolboy correspondence in it. He became the best bicycle rider in Great Britain, holding the championship for every distance from fifty yards to fifty miles. His great race was for the world's championship for fifty miles at Lily Bridge, where he beat out the world's champion John Keen in the last sixty yards. He was the first man to ride continuously the 999 miles from Land's End to John o' Groat's. Then he took up shorthand until he was recognized by Isaac Pitman, the inventor of modern shorthand, as the most rapid writer and accurate student of shorthand in England. Before he was twenty-one he wrote the article on shorthand for the *Encyclopædia Britannica.* His interest in Semitic studies had made him the leading Arabic scholar in England. "Our young master," Noldeke called him, and at the age of thirty he was chosen to succeed Robertson Smith as Lord Almoner's Professor of Arabic in Cambridge University. He had married the daughter of a wealthy London banker, Mr. R. C. L. Bevan, and had every door of scholarship and social opportunity open before him. Then one day he asked himself why he had all this equipment and resource. Why but to use it for his Master and Lord? An invitation came to him from Chinese Gordon to join him in studying the scenes and identifying the sites of Jesus' life in Palestine. What more enticing invitation could a young man of that day have received? But at the same time his friend, Major-General Haig, returning from India, wrote to him of the moral and spiritual need of the tribesmen in southern Arabia and laid this need on his soul. Keith-Falconer responded to his call, equipped and established a mission at Sheikh Othman, and there in less than eighteen months died of Arabian fever, fulfilling, in the grand language of the Wisdom of Solomon, a long time in a short time—one "crowded hour of glorious life."

I remember the impression which Keith-Falconer's death made on the students of that generation, and not his death only but his clean, strong life, a life that surrendered to its Master and so entered into Mastery. How fully he had made Christ Master even in small things his boyhood letters reveal. Here are two written at the age of seventeen from Harrow:

"I must say something about Jesus Christ, because I think He ought never to be left out; and that is the fault I find with parties and balls and theatres: Jesus Christ, Who is the All in All, is utterly left out. It seems very curious, when one comes to think about it, what power the devil has over people, has not he? But that shall not always be so—Lord, hasten the time when Thou shalt reign altogether, and when Thy servants shall serve Thee, and Thy Name shall be upon their foreheads, and when they shall see Thy face—for Jesus' sake."

"Charrington sent me a book yesterday, which I have read. It is called *Following Fully,* . . . about a man who works among the cholera people in London, so hard that he at last succumbs and dies. But every page is full of Jesus Christ, so that I liked it. And I like Charrington, because he is quite devoted to Him, and has really given up all for His glory. I must go and do the same soon: but I don't know." [3]

The Lordship of Jesus Christ must mean to us the enrichment and enlargement of all our life by its passing into His transforming, redeeming, protecting ownership. There life becomes Life, transcends the limits

---

[3] *Cf. Life of Ion Keith-Falconer* by Sinker (Deighdon Bell & Co., London).

of the lower plane and becomes Eternal, mastered by its one true Master into freedom.

The last of these New Testament words for Master is the most distinctive and significant of all—*despotes*. The word implies nothing, however, of our word "despot," with its element of arbitrariness and tyranny. It is used of God and translated "Lord" in Simeon's prayer in the Temple (Luke ii:29) and in the prayers of Peter and John when released by their Jewish rulers (Acts iv:24); and by John in Revelation vi:10. And it is used of human masters in I Timothy vi:1, 2; Titus ii:9 and I Peter ii:18. But thrice it is used of the Lord Jesus, and each time is translated "Master." "Master," however, is a feeble word. "Emperor" would be perhaps our nearest equivalent. Re-read these verses with the word "Emperor" substituted. "Now in a great house there are not only vessels of gold and of silver, but also of wood and of earth; and some unto honour, and some unto dishonour. If a man therefore purge himself from these, he shall be a vessel unto honour, sanctified, meet for the Emperor's use, prepared unto every good work" (II Tim. ii:20, 21). "But there arose false prophets also among the people, as among you also there shall be false teachers, who shall privily bring in destructive heresies, denying even the Emperor that bought them, bringing upon themselves swift destruction" (II Peter ii:1). "For there are certain men crept in privily, even they who were of old written of beforehand unto this condemnation, ungodly men, turning the grace of our God into lasciviousness, and denying our only Emperor and Lord, Jesus Christ" (Jude 4).

Two reminiscences will suffice to set forth the meaning of this Lordship.

Many years ago there was a church in Mercer Street, New York City, known as "The Church of the Strangers." It was a quiet pocket of a street between Broadway and University Place just north of Waverly Place near Washington Square. I lived near by, and one Sunday evening went in to hear Dr. Deems preach. He was a dear old man whose work was done. A green baize curtain hung across the church and the small company who were there sat in the few pews in front of the curtain. I remember of the sermon only an illustration. It was of a French soldier in the Napoleonic wars. He had been shot in the breast and the surgeons were operating on the field. Those were the days before anæsthetics, and the wounded man looked up at the surgeons as they cut in to find the bullet. As the cardiac region was opened up and the man felt the cool air around his heart, as the knife cut closer in, he said haltingly, "Surgeon, if you cut much further—you'll touch—the Emperor." He had him there in his heart. If this poor earthly emperor, how much more the Emperor that bought us!

On the last night of Dr. John Kelman's stay in America, where he so richly served Christ and His Church, I heard him recount the story of his years among us. Of all his experiences, he said one stood out above the rest, and it came to him on his way to New York to take up the pastorate of the Fifth Avenue Church. He had as a fellow passenger the late Dr. Matthew D. Mann, of Buffalo, the famous surgeon who did all that human skill could do to save Mr. McKinley's life after his assassination. I knew Dr. Mann as a dear friend for many years. He was a great fisherman, and he was a devout but very reticent Christian, with a deep love which he found it hard to disclose. Dr. Kelman said that each evening he and Dr. Mann met on the upper deck in a quiet spot behind one of the lifeboats and talked together. Night by night Dr. Mann opened wider his inner heart as they discussed our sad and divided and weary world. On the last evening, at length, Dr. Mann burst forth, "I will tell you, Dr. Kelman, what we need. We need an Emperor. The world needs an Emperor." "An Emperor," Dr. Kelman replied, "for our democratic world?" "Yes," answered Dr. Mann, "an Emperor. And I will tell you His Name; His Name is Jesus Christ. There is no hope until we make Him Emperor."

This is the essence of Christian discipleship—the free acceptance of the Lordship of Christ—Thomas' confession, "My Lord and my God," the glad exclamation of Mary, "My Master." And it is the fundamental need of our modern world. It needs a Lord. It is not competent to be its own master. Its confusion and contention, its groping and bewilderment, its despair and hopelessness, its misery and suffering, its wrong and sin will continue and grow worse until it comes to the great truths so clearly and so boldly spoken by Paul, that the true head of every man is Christ—"that we may be no longer children, tossed to and fro and carried about with every wind of doctrine, by the sleight of men, in craftiness, after the wiles of error; but speaking truth in love, may grow up in all things into Him, Who is the Head, even Christ; from Whom all the body fitly framed and knit together through that which every joint supplieth, according to the working in due measure of each several part, maketh the increase of the body unto the building of itself in love" (Eph. iv:14-16).

VI

WHAT THE SECOND COMING OF CHRIST MEANS TO ME

WHAT is wrong with the Church," writes Professor J. Alexander Findlay in the *British Weekly*, "is that we have discarded doctrines like the Second Advent, which do not fit into the philosophy taught us at school and college; in other words, we have usurped God's prerogatives, and there can be no advance until we have made a fresh submission." This is only a preparatory word.

If we ask the question, What is Christianity? we get many replies. One Christian group answers, A set of facts, of highly accredited historic facts. If we object that this definition will apply just as well to geology, they answer, Yes, but these facts cluster about a Person. A second group would reply, A set of emotions. If we object that the feelings with which we look upon nature or with which we listen to music might be defined in the same way, they answer, Yes, but these emotions centre upon a Person and are in the nature of a personal love. A third group answers, A set of opinions. If we object that this definition would apply as well to materialism, they answer, Yes, but these opinions are beliefs in and about a Person and cluster around a living spirit. A fourth group answers, A code of conduct. If we object that this definition will apply as well to any standard of ethics, they answer, Yes, but this conduct is expressible only in the terms of service of a Person. Each definition resolves in the end into Christ. Christianity is Christ. Dr. Griffith Thomas took this very sentence a generation ago for the title of an admirable little book on the fundamental character of Christianity.

In what sense is Christianity Christ? Christianity is Christ, first, as the historic Saviour and Redeemer. Christianity is Christ, second, as the present Lord and Life of man. Christianity is Christ, third, as the Ideal and Head of humanity. Is that all? We should have a truncated Christianity if that were all, a Christianity very rich and full, but incomplete. Christianity is Christ not alone as the historic Saviour and Redeemer; not alone as the present Lord and Life of man; not alone as the Ideal and Head of a new humanity, the expression of God's desire for every creature—Christianity is also Christ as our coming Master and King. And the hope of Christ's coming again is an integral part of our Christian faith.

We must go back to every one of these four conceptions of Christianity and include Christ's second coming therein. If Christianity is a set of facts, what are its facts? First of all, that Jesus Christ came into this world by way of the manger and the Virgin Birth—the great fact of the lowly Incarnation; that Jesus Christ went out of this world by way of the Cross and the open grave—the great truths of the Atonement and the Resurrection; that the Holy Spirit came into this world as Christ's advocate to abide here as His representative; and that Jesus Christ is coming back again. If Christianity is a set of emotions, what are those emotions? The constraint of the love of a perfect Saviour, but also the desire that He should come again, and the glorious feeling which the prospect of His return awakens. If Christianity is a set of beliefs, what are those beliefs? That Jesus Christ was our Lord; that Jesus Christ is our Lord; yes, more, and that Jesus Christ is to be our returned and victorious Lord. If Christianity is a code of conduct, what are the sanctions of that conduct? Again the constraint of Christ's love, the righteous fear of Christ's judgment, but also the expectation that the Master Whom we serve is coming back again and would find us at our service, faithful to Him for Whom we are to watch and wait.

The hope of Christ's second coming is an integral part of our Christian faith. It is also a necessary part of our Christian faith. It is necessary from the point of view of our Christian faith itself. Christ must come again in order to complete and fulfil His first coming. A Jewess said to a friend who was endeavouring to persuade her that Jesus of Nazareth was the Messiah: "I do not know. If He was, I know He must come again, and when He comes again He will tell us Jews whether He was here before." Christianity is an incomplete, and imperfect, and unfulfilled thing unless the goal of it is the return of Jesus to complete that which He began. The return of Christ is essential to Christianity from the point of view of the inner needs of Christianity for its own completeness. Hugh Martin has characterized it justly in the title of his little book, *The Necessity of the Second Coming*. And that sound scholar and great Christian, Dr. Mullins, wrote: "Properly understood, the Second Coming is the consistent outcome for a religion which began with a historical Incarnation and Resurrection. Christ's person is the centre of God's revelation to men. It is central in our faith, hope, and love. It is central in history. The preaching of the gospel of Christ is the task of Christ's people. God is dealing with men in and through Christ.

Now his personal return to earth is certainly not a conception unrelated to all the above facts. If the religion of Christ is a historical religion, then the consummation may be best expressed in terms of history. The Second Coming is the inevitable historical sequence of the first coming. The two are indissolubly bound together. The Epistle to the Hebrews has expressed this thought very forcibly (Heb. ix:27, 28)."

It is essential to Christianity from the point of view of the personal requirements of our own spiritual lives. We need the hope of Christ's second coming as a buttress to our faith in the supernatural. Even in the days of Simon Peter, when the hope of Christ's return had begun to grow dim, Peter said that men had begun to lose faith in the supernatural and to miss from their lives the sanctions of conduct that came from a supernatural faith, and their naturalism found expression in the question, "Where is the hope of His coming? for all things continue as they were from the beginning of the creation." An old minister in New Jersey confessed to me that after having been in the ministry for many years he found that his Christian faith had died away into sheer naturalism, and that he was preaching to men a simple moral gospel. Then he recovered the hope of Christ's coming. The expectation of that great supernatural future event made all other supernaturalisms easy. We need the hope of Christ's coming to fortify our faith in the supernatural, which cannot be kept alive simply by a belief in supernatural occurrences eighteen hundred years ago. We need it to vivify and to keep quick and active our living Christian faith today. It is easy for Christian faith to die away into what is purely intellectual, historical, external. Men love to have to do with a Christ of ancient history, and they do not like to have to do with a Christ of present life and a Christ of coming judgment. People would rather have Christ wandering up and down through Palestine eighteen centuries past, than testing their present-day lives by the standard of His own, or standing over them as the judge already waiting at the door. The element of expectation is essential to life. We cannot retain pure and fresh and quick our faith in the Christ who died and rose again unless we believe also in the Christ who is reigning now and who is again to come.

Now this necessity of our spiritual life for something to strengthen and make vital to us our faith in the supernatural, this necessity of our personal life to have some truth that will supply the element of prophecy and expectation, is met by Christ's teaching of His own personal coming. It must be confessed that this truth has been ignored and confused among Christians. The doctrine of the Second Coming of Christ is a doctrine which most Christians leave severely alone. Any one who declares his belief in it and who attempts to deal with it will surely suffer for his hardihood. On the one hand he will be attacked by some of those who are convinced that they fully understand the signs of the present time and the sequence of events to come and who draw up schedules. And on the other hand he will be reproached by those who regard the expectation of a personal return of Christ as only a remnant of ancient apocalyptic.

Some Christians simply pass over the teaching of the New Testament on the subject. There is enough else to engross them and other things seem to them more important. One great *Systematic Theology* comprises three volumes of 2,260 pages in all. The chapter on the Second Advent embraces ninety pages, of which only eight deal with "The Personal Advent of Christ," and this chapter begins with the statement: "This is a very comprehensive and very difficult subject. It is intimately allied with all the other great doctrines which fall under the head of eschatology. It has excited so much interest in all ages of the Church, that the books written upon it would of themselves make a library. The subject cannot be adequately discussed without taking a survey of all the prophetic teachings of the Scriptures both of the Old Testament and of the New. This task cannot be satisfactorily accomplished by any one who has not made the study of the prophecies a specialty. The author, knowing that he has no such qualifications for the work, purposes to confine himself in a great measure to a historical survey of the different schemes of interpreting the Scriptural prophecies relating to this subject."[1]

This godly writer sums up the teaching of the New Testament thus: "From all these passages, and from the whole drift of the New Testament, it is plain, (1) That the Apostles fully believed that there is to be a second coming of Christ. (2) That His coming is to be in person, visible and glorious. (3) That they kept this great event constantly before their own minds, and urged it on the attention of the people, as a motive to patience, constancy, joy, and holy living. (4) That the Apostles believed that the second advent of Christ would be attended by the general Resurrection, the final judgment, and the end of the world."

The first three points are clear. The fourth is not clear. And it is in such affirmations as these by some, and their denial by others, that the rich truth of our

---

[1] Charles Hodge, *Systematic Theology,* Vol. III, p. 790 (Scribners).

Lord's Return and its meaning in our experience become confused and lost.

Perhaps we have never been told that Jesus Christ is coming back again. I remember well the first time I went to Northfield many years ago as a sophomore in college. In Hillside Cottage a little group came back to our rooms from a meeting, in which someone had pointed out the New Testament passages promising the return of Jesus Christ. Life seemed altogether changed for some of us in that hour. I discovered that Christ was not resting in the grave at Jerusalem; that Christ was not sitting forever God-remote at the right hand of the Father, but that He was waiting the coming of that glad moment when He was to come back again to all of those "who love His appearing."

Men have neglected this truth out of indifference and carelessness. It has suffered also from exaggerations. Despite Christ's clear warning, men have fixed upon the day of His coming. They have described the events that are to accompany His appearing, and have raised a repugnance to the whole idea of our Lord's return in the minds of many who are repelled by the extremes of "dispensationalism" and the speculations of time-table eschatology.

Many, perhaps, also are averse to this truth because of the scepticism and naturalism that creep into our thought. Men veer off from the supernatural. They tone down their statements of Christ's divinity. Many shrink from the idea of the full, unique deity of Christ and His all-absorbing claims, and they do not like the idea of the miracle of a real returning Saviour who shall come again as once nineteen hundred years ago He went away.

If the supernatural return of Christ is a reality, then

all ground for unbelief or doubt regarding the supernaturalism of the Incarnation is gone. This is one reason why the belief in His Second Coming is, as all who cherish that belief know it to be, the dissolution of every misgiving as to the truth of His Virgin Birth, His miracles and His Resurrection.

Now there cannot be the slightest question as to what the plain, simple declaration of the New Testament is. As clearly as language can express it, and repeated again and again in many forms, the New Testament declares that Jesus is to come back again. The Gospels represent this as the teaching of Jesus. "I will come again" (John xiv:3). "The Son of Man shall come in the glory of the Father" (Matt. xvi:27). "Watch therefore, for ye know not on what day your Lord cometh" (Matt. xxiv:42). "The Son of Man shall come in His glory" (Matt. xxv:31). "Occupy till I come" (Luke xix:13). "Be ye also ready, for in an hour that he think not the Son of Man cometh" (Luke xii:40). "But of that day or that hour knoweth no one, not even the angels in heaven, neither the Son but the Father. Take ye heed, watch and pray: for ye know not when the time is. It is as when a man, sojourning in another country, having left his house, and given authority to his servants to each one his work, commanded also the porter to watch. Watch therefore: for ye know not when the lord of the house cometh, whether at even, or at midnight, or at cock-crowing, or in the morning; lest coming suddenly He find you sleeping. And what I say unto you I say unto all, Watch" (Mark xiii:32-37).

The Book of Acts begins with a declaration which would seem to be beyond the possibility of misunderstanding: "And while they were looking steadfastly into heaven as He went, behold, two men stood by them in white apparel; who also said, Ye men of Galilee, why stand ye looking into heaven? this Jesus, who was received up from you into heaven, shall so come in like manner as ye beheld Him going into heaven" (Acts i:10, 11).

Almost every writer in the New Testament affirms his faith in our Lord's future return. "He shall appear" they say (I John ii:28, iii:2; I Peter v:4; Col. iii:4; Heb. ix:28). Again and again they refer to "His appearing," not His past appearing, but His coming again (I Tim. vi:14; II Tim. iv:1, 8; Titus ii:13; I Peter 1:7). And "appearing" in these passages does not mean Christ's invisible spiritual companionship (cf. II Tim. i:10). It means His personal return, something that is to be looked for and seen. It is a revelation (I Peter i:5, 7, 13; I Cor. i:7, 8; Rom. v: 18; II Thess. i:7, ii:6, 8). It is a coming, and our Bibles so translate the words of the original Greek (I Cor. i:7, xv:23; I Thess. ii:19, iii:13, iv:15, v:23; II Thess. ii:1, 8; James v:7, 8; II Peter i:16, iii:4, 12; I John ii:28). "He shall come" (II Thess. i:10; Heb. x:37; II Peter iii:10).

So clear and so pervasive was this faith of the New Testament Church that no one can deny that these first Christians were expecting and longing for Christ's return. Indeed it is held that they believed He would return in their lifetime and that accordingly they interpreted the doctrines of Christianity and fashioned their lives on the basis of this belief. It would seem that some did hold this faith and that some indeed even feared that Christ had already returned and that they had missed Him (II Thess. ii:1-3). But it cannot be maintained on the evidence found in the New Testament, that the Apostles and the primitive Church went any further than the Lord's teaching justified. They were to live as men who were waiting and ready for Christ's return, but they were not to fix a time or to be confused by those who proclaimed His imminence (Matt. xxiv:5, 23; Mark xiii:6, 21-23; Luke xxi:8, 9).

Now these promises of Christ and of Christ's Word cannot be exhausted by any mere spiritualized interpretation. We believe that Jesus Christ comes in death. No one need hesitate to acknowledge that in every great event of life that brings to us the message of God, Jesus Christ comes to us. It is the most blessed truth that Christ has come to us and is with us now. But it becomes impossible any longer to indicate thought by human speech, if these words of the New Testament are emptied of their actual primary significance in this way.

We cannot exhaust the promise of Christ's coming by death. Death is our great foe. "The last enemy that shall be overcome," says Paul, "is death." Consistently, from beginning to end, death is set before us as a certain experience, but never as a "blessed hope." Can you apply to death all the sweet words that are spoken of the coming of Christ, for which we are told to look? Paul draws the sharp distinction between them in the first five verses of the fifth chapter of II Corinthians. He points out that there is a world of difference between dying and Christ's coming. "We that are in this tabernacle," he says, "do groan, being burdened: not for that we would be unclothed,"—that is, die and go into the grave, and our spirits be separated from our bodies—"not that we would be unclothed, but clothed upon, that what is mortal might be swallowed up of life," that we might have the new life which Christ will give us when He comes (Phil. iii:20, 21). The Apostles never dreamed of confusing death and Christ's coming. Jesus said to Peter about John on the day when He and Peter were walking by the shores of the Sea of Galilee, "If I will that he tarry till I come, what is that to thee?" "Then went the saying abroad," says John, "that that disciple should not die." The Apostles instantly interpreted the hint that a man might live until Christ came back again as a promise that he should not die. From beginning to end, the promises of the New Testament about Christ's coming mean nothing if the words about His coming are exhausted in the meeting between our souls and Him when we go to Him in death, blessed as that meeting is.

Some have held that the promise of Christ's return was fulfilled in the fall of Jerusalem. Take one passage and exchange the language and see. Take the closing verses of I Thessalonians i, for example, where Paul speaks to the Thessalonians of their having "turned from idols to serve the living and true God, and to wait for His Son from heaven, whom He raised from the dead, even Jesus." Read that this way: "Ye turned from idols to serve the living and true God, and to wait for the fall of Jerusalem." Try the substitution elsewhere and see how it makes the words of the New Testament meaningless and absurd. One of the Gospels, at least, was written after the holy city had been destroyed. If those prophecies had been fulfilled in the destruction of Jerusalem, we may be sure that there would have been some allusion thereto.

We cannot exhaust the promise of Christ's coming again by any reference of it to personal spiritual life. It is to be acknowledged regarding prophecy, when we think of the very essence of prophecy, that all through life men should be fulfilling it in themselves. But every spiritual fulfilment in any life of the promise of Christ's presence is only a fresh witness to its large, and rich, and complete fulfilment in the day when every eye shall see Him, and He shall come back again even as He went away. "The character of the predictions in the New Testament," says Dr. Charles Hodge, "does not admit of their being made to refer to any spiritual coming of Christ or to the constant progress of His Church."

The teaching of the New Testament about the return of Christ is sometimes presented as resting on the word "parousia" or "presence," and the passages are then construed to mean that Christ's presence with the Church and in the life of the believers is the fulfilment of the promise of His coming. But that coming is described in the New Testament by other words than "parousia" and these words cannot be considered as fulfilled in our Lord's spiritual presence.

There is the simple word "come." Can it be interpreted to refer only to Christ's presence in the soul or in the Church? "Ye know not what hour your Lord doth come" (Matt. xxiv:42). "The Son of Man shall come in the glory of the Father" (Matt. xvi:27). "In an hour that ye think not the Son of Man cometh" (Luke xii:35-40). And when He said, "Occupy till I come," and in establishing the Lord's Supper, "Ye do show forth the Lord's death till He come," did He mean that our duty of occupation was fulfilled when we had His spiritual presence with us and that thereafter also we need no longer observe the Sacrament? And does Christ's presence in the heart fulfil the terms of the declaration of the two men in white at the Ascension? "This Jesus, who was received up from you into heaven, shall so come in like manner as ye beheld Him going into heaven" (Acts i:11).

And Christ's coming is described also by the word "epiphaneia" or "appearance." This word does not mean "spiritual presence." It is used by Paul of Christ's first advent (II Tim. i:10). And in the same sense it is used of His second advent (I Tim. vi:14; II Tim. iv:8; Titus ii:13). And the early disciples, who surely had Christ in their hearts, never supposed that that experience was the equivalent of His coming. They speak of His appearance as a future thing (Col. iii:4; I John ii:28, iii:2; I Peter v:4). "He shall appear a second time" (Heb. ix:28).

In the same way they speak of a revelation (apokalupsis), an unveiling of Christ that is to come, a revelation which is identified with His Second Coming (II Thess. i:7-10; I Peter i:5, 7, 13; Rom. v:18; I Cor. i:7, 8).

Once again, the attitude of the early Church was one of waiting and looking for something future, not yet fulfilled in their very real and blessed experience of the spiritual presence of their Saviour: "Waiting for the revelation of our Lord Jesus Christ" (I Cor. i:7; *cf.* II Thess. iii:5; I Thess. i:10). "Looking for the blessed hope and appearing of the glory of the great God and our Saviour Jesus Christ" (Titus ii:13; *cf.* II Peter iii:12; Matt. xxiv:50; Luke xii:46; Phil. iii:20; Heb. ix:28).

And even in the case of the word "parousia," it is impossible to fit the idea of Christ's present spiritual presence into the New Testament passages where the word occurs. The early Christians knew all that we know about that presence in their hearts and they still looked for the "parousia" in the sense of a future coming (I Cor. xv:23; I Thess. ii:19, iii:13, iv:15, v:23; II Thess. ii:1, 8; James v:7, 8; II Peter iii:4, 12; I John ii:28). If "parousia" means simply the presence of Christ or His life in the Church after Pentecost why should the word appear only in the Epistles and after the experience of the coming of the Holy Spirit and be referred constantly to a future event? Christ's coming is nowhere spoken of in the Gospels as a "parousia," among all their references to Christ's Second Coming, except in Matthew xxiv:3, 27, 37, 39. If the promised "parousia" was Christ's spiritual presence one would have expected to find the word used before the Resurrection and Pentecost, and with reference only to that spiritual experience and not to a future, objective event.

This was the faith and the hope of the first Christians and we cannot read the New Testament without seeing what a place it filled in their lives as a confirmation of faith and as an inspiration of conduct. As Dr. Mullins wrote:

"There are at least two ways in which the expectation of Christ's near return served the ends of the kingdom of God among these early Christians. First, it was a moral and spiritual incentive of the highest value. The age was one of great trial and suffering. The thought of Christ's return to power was a source of great consolation, and inspired to zeal and devotion. Whenever it led to extravagant or fanatical forms of conduct, these were at once corrected by the apostles. The belief was turned to moral and spiritual account, to the uses of sobriety and of holy living. Secondly, the expectation of Christ's personal return gave unity to the faith of believers. The Christ who had already come was the Christ who would come again. If Christ had abandoned the world forever after the ascent from Olivet, a great blank would have been left in the future for His followers. What is to be the outcome of Christian effort? How is the ongoing of history to terminate? What is the dominant force in the history of the world? Questions like these would have been left without satisfactory answer apart from the doctrine of the Second Coming. His return in glory was thus a truth which held Him closely bound to the fortunes of His people on earth. For then He was ever thus the Christ who stood within the shadow 'keeping watch above his own.' These same principles apply to Christians of today under the changed circumstances of the world. Any age of self-indulgence needs the same stimulus to holy living. There has been vast ingenuity and arduous labour on the part of scholars in dealing with this element in the religion of Christ as set forth in the New Testament. But there has often been a notable lack of spiritual insight and of sympathy with the genius of the Christian faith. Jesus Christ as Revealer of God and Redeemer of men fills the horizon of the Christian believer, the horizon of the future as well as of the present and the past. The whole of the personal life in its relation to God and to history must be construed in terms of the personal relation to Christ Himself." [2]

And all that this "blessed hope" meant to the early Christians it means to us. It means, first of all, that our long-sundered ties are to be united again. "If we believe that Jesus died and rose again, even so them also which sleep in Jesus will God bring with Him. For we that are alive and remain shall not prevent them which are asleep. For the Lord Himself shall descend from heaven with a shout, with the voice of the archangel, and with the trump of God, and the dead in Christ shall rise first: then we which are alive and remain shall be caught up together with them in the cloud, to meet the Lord in the air: and so shall we ever be with the Lord" (I Thess. iv:14-17). When Hugh Beaver died many years ago there was a little group of railroad men in a town on the banks of the Susquehanna who had learned to love him, who as

[2] E. Y. Mullins, *The Christian Religion.*

soon as they learned of his death, turned to their Bibles and found those verses, and telegraphed them to his mother. They were the greatest words that came to her, as she looked forward to that day when all the sundered ties are to be knit together again, when all the broken friendships are to be woven once more, when all the dissevered homes are to be rebound, and when all the lives that for a little while we are obliged to lose sight of here, are gathered up to be no more separated forever. The coming of Christ means the glorification of all our human relationships, the knitting up of all our severed human ties, the making permanent and eternal of all our human loves and affections.

It means our emancipation from the influence of outer evil. George Adam Smith gives a fresh translation of one of the verses of the eleventh chapter of Isaiah. It is the chapter that speaks of the shoot coming out of the stock of Jesse, and one verse is translated in the Revised Version, "His delight shall be in the fear of the Lord." Dr. Smith points out that the literal Hebrew reading is "He shall draw breath in the fear of the Lord." It was a prophecy of the Messiah. He was to be free from the contagion of the carnal atmosphere in which we live. He drew all his breath, not in the miasma of our lustful life, but in the pure, clean, ever-enduring fear of the Lord. And the teaching of the New Testament is this, that when Jesus comes back, we, too, like Him, shall be free from the power of these external allurements to sin, from all these incitements to evil, all lawlessness. The very prince of wickedness himself is to be slain by the breath of His mouth, and by the manifestation of His power. "We know," says St. John, "that when He shall appear we shall be like Him, for we shall see Him as He is."

And not only does Jesus by His coming mean to deliver us from the outer evil; by His coming He means to deliver us also from the inner source of temptation and allurement. It is not without but within, as Jesus said, that the great source of evil is to be found: "There is nothing from without the man, that going into him can defile him; but the things which proceed out of the man are those that defile the man" (Mark vii:15). "For out of the heart come forth evil thoughts, murders, adulteries, fornications, thefts, false witness, railings: these are the things which defile the man; but to eat with unwashen hands defileth not the man" (Matt. xv:19, 20). Professor Bruce, in his volume on *St. Paul's Conception of Christianity,* refers to Paul's allusions to his own personal temptations as indicating the warfare which even he had to wage. Why was it that Paul was so constantly speaking of the temptations of the flesh, why did he make such lists of the sins that soil men's lives, why tell the Corinthians that he was obliged to buffet his own body and bring it under? Paul knew what it was to be tempted in his body and in the expectation of Christ's coming he found the hope of his deliverance. Twice at least he speaks of this. First to the Corinthians: "For we know that if the earthly house of our tabernacle be dissolved, we have a building from God, a house not made with hands, eternal, in the heavens. For verily in this we groan, longing to be clothed upon with our habitation which is from heaven: if so be that being clothed we shall not be found naked. For indeed we that are in this tabernacle do groan, being burdened; not for that we would be unclothed, but that we would be clothed upon, that what is mortal may be swallowed up of life" (II Cor. v:1-4). And again to the Philippians: "For our citizenship is in heaven; whence also we wait for a Saviour, the Lord Jesus Christ: Who shall fashion anew the body of our humiliation, that it may be conformed to the body of His glory, according to the working whereby He is able even to subject all things unto Himself" (Phil. iii:20, 21). Paul longed for the day when Christ should come back and give him in exchange for all that which he carried with him daily, with its daily temptations, a body like Christ's own, of purity, of stainlessness and of glory.

And the coming of Christ means not these things only. It means the redemption of all our human life. We recall the mighty passage in Paul's Epistle to the Romans, the eighth chapter, in which he links all creation to us and suggests that just as Jesus Christ is our mediator, we are the mediator of the beasts; that as Jesus Christ brought us holiness and peace, so the dumb creation waits for its redemption until the sons of God are revealed in us. "For the earnest expectation of the creation waiteth for the redemption of the sons of God," Paul wrote. "For the creation was subjected to vanity, not of its own will, but by reason of Him Who subjected it in hope that the creation itself shall also be delivered from the bondage of corruption into the liberty of the glory of the children of God. For we know that the whole creation groaneth and travaileth in pain together until now, and not only so, but ourselves also, which have the first fruits of the spirit, even we ourselves groan within ourselves waiting for our adoption"—which has not been completed as yet—"to wit, the redemption of our body." Deliverance from sin, from the possibility of sin, from the outside allurement to sin, from the internal inclination to sin, the knitting up of all the severed loves of earth—these things the coming of Jesus Christ will mean.

Now do not let us be confused or misled by any doubts or disputes of men, by misguiding or misleading speculations as to the manner and time of Christ's coming. It is enough for us to know just what the Bible states and no more. It tells us plainly all that it is necessary for us to know about the manner of His coming. The same Christ is coming back Who went away. "This same Jesus, which is today taken up from you into heaven, shall so come again in like manner as ye have seen Him go." It is the personal Jesus Who is to come back visibly to us, Who is to come back unexpectedly in such an hour as we think not, Who is to come back not unexpectedly only, but suddenly. Luke preserves for us the words of Christ in which he likens the suddenness of His coming to the flashing of the lightning from the east to the west. "As thou seest the lightning flash from one quarter of the heaven to another, even so shall the coming of the Son of Man be." Matthew preserves the teaching by which Jesus likened the suddenness of His coming to the quickness of the coming of the flood in the days of Noah. "For as in those days that were before the flood they were eating and drinking, marrying and giving in marriage, until the day when Noah entered into the ark, and they knew not, until the flood came and took them all away; so shall be the coming of the Son of Man. Watch, therefore, for ye know not the day or the hour when the Lord shall come." These words tell us all that we need to know about the time of His coming. Jesus Himself said that He did not know when He would come: "Of that day and of that hour knoweth no man, no, not the angels of God, neither the Son, but the Father only." When He talked with His disciples with reference to the time, He told them that all that was required of them was that they should watch: "Watch, for in an hour that you think not the Son of Man cometh."

What made it plain to them that they were not to nullify His teaching by any human additions was this command to watch. They were not to kill all significance of meaning in His promise by interposing any long period of time or order of events that must transpire before He could come again. There are people who tell us that the whole world must be converted before Christ comes back. When will that be? We have not converted a single town in America as yet. Jesus did not say that every soul in the world must be converted to Him before He came. He made it plain that the tares and the wheat were to grow up together until the harvest. He made it plain that just as there were wicked people in the days of Noah when the flood came, so there would be sinning men in the day when He came back. He went so far once even as to put it in the form of a question: "When the Son of Man cometh will He find faith on the earth?" And the teaching of the whole New Testament is that evil will last in the world until the day when Christ comes to slay it with the glory of His appearing.

We know that the Apostles expected His return. Bible scholars agree that the early Christians actually were watching for Him. Many of them think that the Apostles believed that Jesus Christ would come in their lifetime. Not so, but we know that the Apostles thought that He might come in their lifetime. "Be patient therefore, brethren, until the coming of the Lord. Behold, the husbandman waiteth for the precious fruit of the earth, being patient over it, until it receive the early and latter rain. Be ye also patient; establish your hearts: for the coming of the Lord is at hand" (James v:7, 8). "Yet a little while," said the writer of the Epistle to the Hebrews, "yet a little while, and He that shall come will come, and will not tarry."

If we are looking in our Christian lives for the most practical and life-moulding truth, surely it is here. There is hardly any truth taught in the New Testament that is more constantly appealed to, scarcely even the truth of Christ's death upon the Cross, scarcely even the truth of Christ's Resurrection from the grave—hardly any truth is more constantly appealed to than this truth of Christ's Second Coming as influencing and moulding conduct.

Consider it in the matter of simple, personal holiness. "And now, little children," writes John (I John ii:28), "and now, little children, abide in Him; that when He shall appear, we may have confidence, and not be ashamed before Him at His coming." And all through the epistles of Paul, we find him appealing to the expectation of Christ's coming as a motive for making life blameless and clean. "Now may our God and Father Himself, and our Lord Jesus direct our way unto you, to the end that He may establish your hearts unblamable in holiness before our God and Father at the coming of our Lord Jesus with all His saints." "And ye are dead, and your lives are hid with Christ in God. When Christ, Who is our life, shall be manifested, then shall we also with Him be manifested in glory. Put to death therefore"—the "therefore" connected at once with the hope of Christ's coming—"put to death therefore your members which are upon the earth; fornication, uncleanness, passion, evil desire and covetousness, which is idolatry." We are looking for something that will purge our lives clean. "Behold what manner of love the Father hath bestowed upon us, that we should be called children of God. For this cause the world knoweth us not, because it knew Him not. Beloved, now are we children of God, and it is not yet made manifest what we shall be. We know that, when He shall be manifested, we shall be like Him; for we shall see Him even as He is. And every one that hath this hope set on Him purifieth himself, even as He is pure." The next time temptation comes, let us fix our mind on the thought of Christ's coming. No one can do an unclean and unholy thing in the eager expectancy of Christ's coming. He that hath this hope in Him will purify himself, even as Christ is pure.

We need the hope of Christ's coming to help us to form right and kind judgments. There is a bad instinct within us that leads us when we are talking about a person to pick out some fault. Something has been said commendatory of a man, and we say, "Yes, but—yes, but he has this weakness, he has that fault, he has this defect." It is too easy for us to be harsh and un-Christian in our judgments. Nothing will deliver us from these so well as the expectation of Christ's return. "Wherefore," writes Paul in the fifth verse of the fourth chapter of First Corinthians, "wherefore, judge nothing before the time until the Lord come, Who will both bring to light the hidden things of darkness, and make manifest the counsels of the heart; and then shall each man have his praise of God." My judgment of you, your judgment of me is nothing. The only judgment that is of avail is the judgment that He shall pass when He comes. Let judgment wait until then. Meanwhile let us love.

The truth of Christ's coming is set before us as the most powerful motive for winning men. "What is our hope," writes Paul in one of his epistles to the Thessalonians, "or joy, or crown of glorying? Are not even ye, before our Lord Jesus at His coming? For ye are our glory and our joy." Very lonesome and desolate we shall feel if we must greet Him alone. Happy and content will we be in that day if we can have someone by the hand, and when He comes can greet Him and say, "Lord, here is my friend. I did not want to come to meet You alone; I asked my friend, that he and I might meet You together when You came." One glory of life in the day of Christ's appearing will be the men, whom out of darkness we may have helped to lead into His marvellous light.

And what more powerful motive to fidelity in daily duty could men find than the expectation of Christ's coming? It is to this that Paul appeals in the last chapter of his last epistle. "I charge thee, Timothy," he says, "in the sight of God and of Jesus Christ, Who shall judge the quick and the dead, and by His appearing and His kingdom; preach the word; be instant in season and out of season." This is the truth that Jesus was enforcing upon His disciples when He held before them the expectation of His coming and said, "Know this; if the man of the house had known in what watch the thief would come, he would have watched and would not have suffered his house to be broken through. Therefore be ye also ready, for in an hour that ye think not the Son of Man cometh." "Who then is that faithful and wise servant, whom his lord has set over his household to give them food in due season? Blessed is that servant whom his lord when he cometh shall find so doing." We do our work better, more honestly, more diligently, more devotedly, because we are expecting Him.

With many the truth of the Second Coming of Christ is discredited by the controversy between premillennialists and postmillennialists over the passage in Revelation xx:1-10. But this is the only mention in the Bible of the "millennium." And there is no warrant for slighting one of the clearest, plainest, most central doctrines of the New Testament because of the difficulty arising from this one great picturesque symbol. Dr. Mullins has dealt with this with his customary wisdom and courage:

"The passage in Revelation xx:1-10 has been given too great prominence in the doctrine of last things by both sides in the millennial controversy. If it is taken literally in all details, it certainly seems to teach the premillennial view in part. But it limits the number of saints who reign with Christ to martyrs. A misgiving also arises as to the place of the thousand-year reign. Nowhere in the vision (ver. 4-10) is it said that these martyred saints reign with Christ on this earth a thousand years. The seer does not say where it occurs. Throughout the book of Revelation John passes at will from heaven to earth and back again. The visions are symbolic in the highest degree in combination with elements that are literal as well. It is at least hazardous to make a single passage like this determinative for the interpretation of a great mass of Scriptures which are not symbolic or highly figurative in form. Yet this is done by both schools. The millennium is the central issue. Everything turns on this.

"Secondly, the teaching of the Old and New Testaments

alike is the ultimate triumph of God's kingdom on earth. Nothing could well be clearer than this, even in the book of Revelation. All the stages of the vision move gradually forward through conflict to the final dénouement in the descent of the city of God to this earth. But no system of interpretation has yet been found which can trace successfully the meaning of all the details. The message of the book is the ultimate triumph. Inspired by this hope and conviction we may face our tasks as Christians.

"Thirdly, both the pre- and the postmillennial theories leave many insoluble problems. The postmillennialist certainly has an impossible task in trying to find a place in his conception of the future for the New Testament attitude of constant expectancy for the coming of the Christ. The premillennialist overloads his programme of the future so that one staggers under the burden. Both make a great mass of literal passages subordinate and tributary to one passage in a symbolic context in a highly figurative book.

"Fourthly, one event occupies the central place in the vision of the future throughout the New Testament from Matthew to Revelation. That event is the Second Coming of Christ. All else is subordinate and tributary to that. Side by side with it are descriptions of gradual growth and of sudden catastrophes in the coming kingdom. There are comings in historical events, and the one great coming. There are great delays and great sufferings, and there are glorious and sudden triumphs. There is no sort of question as to at least one resurrection, and one judgment, and one eternal kingdom. There is no clear assurance that there must be a thousand years of perfect piety on earth before Christ returns. There is no clear guaranty that He will reign literally on earth with all the risen saints a thousand years before the final judgment.

"In the fifth place, it follows that Christians should cultivate the New Testament attitude of expectancy. We should ever be as men who look for their Lord, because He commanded it, and because we love and trust Him, and because all the future would be blank without Him. He is the key which unlocks for us the hidden things of the coming ages. But we should not become absorbed in apocalyptic calculations and speculations. We should not be so assured of the programme of the unrevealed future that we 'begin to beat our fellow servants' because they do not accept our particular interpretation (Matt. xxiv:49). We should not attempt to fix dates or insist too greatly upon detailed programmes. We should be faithful in every detail of duty. We should ever watch against temptation and pray for divine strength. We should cultivate a passion for righteousness, individual and social. We should work while it is day, knowing that the night cometh when no man can work. We should be so eager for the coming of our Lord, that if He should come tomorrow we would not be taken by surprise. We should so hold ourselves in restraint, that if His return should be delayed a thousand or ten thousand years, we would not be disappointed. And our hearts should be ever filled with joy at the prospect of His coming and the certain triumph of His kingdom." [3]

In the *Life and Letters of John A. Broadus,* one of the greatest scholars and saints which America has produced, are two letters referring to the subject of our Lord's return and the issue between pre- and postmillennialists.

The first of these is from Dr. A. J. Gordon, of Boston, to Dr. Broadus, dated November 12, 1878:

"In speaking of the theological seminaries I only gave expression to the general impression. All in this part of the country are strongly and avowedly postmillennial, and the other view is for the most part looked upon with great disfavour. I was greatly delighted and surprised to learn your sentiments. . . .

"I accept with thanks your admonition in regard to 'allegorical interpretation.' I hope I may not go astray or lead others astray. . . .

"When a college president standing in the orthodox ranks can write such words as these I give from his letter to me: 'The coming of Christ was the primitive hope, I grant, and it was the most egregiously mistaken hope into which the

[3] E. Y. Mullins, *The Christian Religion.*

Church ever fell. I do not believe that Christ will ever come to earth in bodily form,' ought not other men of learning to tell what they believe in regard to 'that blessed hope?' "

The second is a letter from Dr. Broadus to Dr. E. Y. Mullins, who later succeeded Dr. Broadus as President of the Southern Baptist Theological Seminary at Louisville, dated January 27, 1894:

"I cannot complain of inquiries about my opinions as given in books and lectures, and of course I am glad to hear from you on any subject.

"I am neither a Pre-milliennarian nor a Post-millennarian, in the usual sense of those terms. I think that the popular view, which I was accustomed in youth to hold in a vague way, that, before the coming of our Lord, there will be a thousand years of universal and perfect Christian piety, is simply impossible in presence of the numerous strong statements made by the Saviour and the apostles that we must be always looking for His coming, and that it will be, as to many persons, wholly unexpected. If there were a period in which all mankind were perfect Christians, surely the world would know just when that period begins, and just when a thousand years of it are about to end, and so all the world would be looking for the Saviour's coming, prepared for it; and this is just the opposite of what the Saviour Himself and His apostles have declared. I believe, therefore, that we ought to be all the time looking for our Lord's coming, and trying to be ready for it. I should not be amazed to see it tomorrow. I have no absolute assurance that it will be this side of a hundred thousand years. I only know that we ought to be trying so to live as to be ready when He comes. I do not know what the thousand years in the book of Revelation mean. The programmes which some writers have drawn up, to be carried out at His coming by our Lord, seem to me quite unwarranted. They rest upon very doubtful interpretations of very obscure expressions. The calculations that He is going to come at a certain time seem to me forbidden by His own statement that the day and hour is unknown to the angels in heaven and was unknown even to His own human mind. So, then, I cannot declare myself in sympathy with the calculations and the programmes of Pre-millennarians. I confine myself to what is clearly taught by the Saviour and His apostles, and we ought to be looking for His Second Coming and trying to be ready for it." [4]

Another objection often made to belief in our Lord's Return is that those who believe in it are pessimists, that they do not believe in the Holy Spirit and His work, that their looking for Christ cuts the nerve of their missionary endeavour. On the contrary, Christ's Second Coming is the source not of discouragement but of glorious hope. It is the Holy Spirit Who declares the truth and keeps it alive. And from the beginning this doctrine has been one of the most powerful and fruitful of motives to evangelism at home and to missionary effort to evangelize the world. "And this gospel of the kingdom shall be preached in the whole world for a testimony unto all the nations; and then shall the end come" (Matt. xxiv:14).

The Second Coming of Christ is in a true sense the base and the crown of the missionary undertaking. It is the guarantee of a supernatural gospel which refuses to be identified with secular civilization because all secular civilization is to be transcended by the Kingdom of God. As Karl Hartenstein said at the International Student Conference at Basle in September, 1935:

"We are confronted by a double and appalling fact. On the one hand, just those peoples in which Gospel and independent civilization entered upon the closest alliance with each other—that is, the peoples of the West—have most sorely squandered and destroyed the Divine heritage of the Gospel. Secularism is the end of an alliance which certainly

[4] *Life and Letters of John A. Broadus,* by A. T. Robertson.

came into being from the beginning not without God's permission and as a likeness of a Divine ordinance of creation. But the alliance is at an end. And what we are experiencing at the heart of the West is the coming of a free Church—free from the powers of civilization, nationality and State, free for a plain and clear presentation of the Gospel, a witness to an approaching new order of all things, a symbol of the revolutionizing force of the Gospel, which cannot rest until the Kingdom of God be come. Here there is granted to our generation a knowledge of the decisive fact that even the closest connection between Church and civilization, between Christianity and nationality, still remains only patchwork, and is threatened at all times by the powers of a humanity which dares to set itself in the place of God. Certainly that alliance too between Church and civilization will not have been in vain for the new Kingdom of God. And how that will appear in the light of eternity is beyond our ken.

"On the other hand, we are confronted by the appalling fact that this process of secularization is irresistibly harassing the peoples of all the world. The heathen civilizations are not in a position to guard themselves against it, or even to make it fruitful for their own life. Therefore Missions are more and more meeting with that spiritually and culturally speaking appalling desert, in which the Church of Jesus Christ, under the strongest pressure from the world, is able to maintain itself among the nations only under the sign of the Cross and of suffering.

"Both facts: the end of the alliance in the West, and the destruction of the heathen religious civilizations, point us powerfully beyond the ultimate limits of earthly history. It is becoming evident to us today that the Gospel is ultimately not a cement and binding material for a dying world and civilization, but a dynamite and explosive in view of a complete re-ordering of all things, when the Day comes which makes all things clear, when the Lord comes Who makes all things new. It is therefore the decisive task of Missions, without prejudice to the important tasks—of implanting and rooting the Gospel in the nations—of which we have already spoken, to make clear to the Church of all nations the eschatological Message, and to make petition for its awakening in their own midst. It is increasingly true that we can carry on Missions among the nations only in the expectation of the new Kingdom in which God Himself is the Lord. Only then will the ultimate mystery be disclosed, as to what significance the work of civilization and the political formation of the individual nations have had in the plan of God. That we prepare the way for this Kingdom by the ministry of the Word, endure under the Cross of the anti-Christian world powers, and believe unshakably in the victory of Jesus Christ: that is the essential task of Missions."

And Hugh Martin, in his little book, *The Necessity of the Second Coming,* published by the British Student Christian Movement, discerns that the world's one hope and the end of all our work is our Lord's Return:

"What we see now is an unfinished conflict. Evil is in opposition to the reign of God, and God's love manifest in Christ strives to vanquish it. It is not a matter of indifference what the outcome of that conflict will be. A permanent moral dualism is not ethical. It is atheistic. The very distinction between right and wrong involves the conviction of the ultimate triumph of the right. It is just because the Bible is so uncompromising on the side of righteousness that it lays so much stress on eschatology. The moral order must be vindicated. 'The Christian doctrine of a final judgment is not the putting of an arbirtary term to the course of history; it is a doctrine without which history ceases to be capable of moral construction.'

"This position is sometimes challenged; goodness is good even if it is defeated, and it is mere selfishness—exalted but still selfish—to be overmuch concerned about the ultimate verdict. But the goodness of a good man is not self-contained. It expresses itself in—and to a large extent consists of—his impact upon the outside world of men. If he is good he will inevitably strive to the best of his ability for the universalizing of the good in human affairs, for the Kingdom of God.

"If the universe is such that this labour is foredoomed to failure, his effort, and therefore much of his goodness, ceases to be worth while. It is sometimes argued—for example, by T. H. Huxley and Bertrand Russell—that the universe in which the moral ideals have somehow arisen is none the less as a whole inherently hostile or apathetic to them. We are called to fight with grim heroism a losing battle. This summons is not without a certain splendour, but besides raising difficult questions as to the ultimate source of human idealism, it inevitably impairs the very goodness of the good will itself.

"If the ideal world toward which our goodness impels us to strive is unattainable, in proportion as we believe that, we shall inevitably slacken our efforts and turn to a self-centred life. For self-sacrifice is only reasonable, and therefore justifiable, in the long run, on the basis that it will not ultimately be fruitless. Christianity calls to self-sacrifice, to self-denying service. It finds supreme value there, apart from any system of external rewards and punishments. But it also insists that all true self-sacrifice is creative of a world of goodness and gladness. It denies that the end of our striving is a delusive dream. It declares that the universe is friendly. Hinduism and Buddhism deny this, or are doubtful, but the ultimate triumph of God's will is of the very essence of Christianity.

"There is to be a Day of Reckoning, a Last Day, a Day of the Lord, a Day of Judgment. Belief in God—or at least in the God and Father of our Lord Jesus Christ—involves a climax to the present stage of human history. There can be no dispute that Jesus enforces this doctrine. The universe is so made and governed that right will be proved right, though no doubt much of the imagery associated with the Day of Judgment is inadequate. Right and wrong have abiding consequences. Sin is not conquered by the destruction of the sinner, but only by his transformation. The Judge is Jesus and love has the last word. No mere display of omnipotent power and external catastrophe can be a worthy vindication of Christ's cause. Love must reach its goal by the ways of love.

"Again, this triumph cannot be relegated to heaven alone.

'If this life be not a real fight in which something is eternally gained for the universe by success, it is no better than a game of private theatricals from which one may withdraw at will. But it feels like a real fight—as if there were something really wild in the universe which we with all our idealities and faithfulnesses are needed to redeem; and first of all to redeem our own hearts from atheisms and fears.' The victory must be where the battle is. The Bible—both Old Testament and New Testament—insists that the Kingdom is to come on earth as well as in heaven. That surely is part of what is meant by the picture of the return of Christ to earth in glory and triumph. The kingdoms of this world shall become the Kingdom of our God and of His Christ. It is His will to establish here a redeemed society—not merely to pluck saved individuals out of a wicked and perishing world. In striving for social regeneration we are not following a will-o'-the-wisp. 'Again, if the dead still take an interest in this earth—and at the least they cannot but be affected by the moral quality of those who keep leaving this world to enter the society of which they are members—there is a sense in which "they without us shall not be made perfect," since the full achievement of the glory of heaven must wait for the complete regeneration of earth.' The Kingdom must come 'on both sides of death.'

"And this triumph is directly associated with the person of Christ. That surely must be so if we give Him the place which the New Testament and the faith of the Church have always given Him. God has 'made known to us the mystery of His will . . . to sum up all things in Christ, the things in the heavens and the things upon the earth' (Eph. i:9, 10). We are not bound to accept the imagery of apocalyptic, and imagination fails—it must fail—to picture the event, necessarily without parallel in human experience. How it shall be we do not know and cannot imagine. But it will be in some such association with this person as can best be described as His coming again.

"We must not, as some have done, isolate eschatology from the rest of the Christian Gospel, but without eschatology that Gospel is not complete. The doctrine of the Second Coming is no mere outworn trapping of Jewish thought, to be discarded in our enlightened times, no unpractical and unworthy matter of speculation. It is of the essence of our faith. It expresses the Christian assurance of victory. It proclaims that ultimate triumph of good which is the justification of our trust in God.

"And when the strife is fierce, the warfare long,
Steals on the ear the distant triumph song
And hearts are brave again, and arms are strong.
Hallelujah!

Jesus taught us to pray in full assurance of faith: 'Thy Kingdom come, Thy will be done on earth as it is in heaven.' The triumph of the cause of Christ is more sure than tomorrow's dawn."

There are two elements in the teaching of Jesus which have sometimes been allowed to confuse the minds of Christians with regard to the simple truth of Christ's Second Coming. One is His unfolding of the future in the great passages in Matthew xxiv, xxv (*cf.* Mark xiii and Luke xxi), and the other is His doctrine of the Kingdom of God. Regarding the former, it is enough to say that Jesus was looking out from that one time and place across the whole of history including His death, the fall of Jerusalem, the unfolding of the ages and the coming of the end, and that He did not intend to furnish a schedule or to mark sharp periods in time. We can afford to await the explanation of what was dark if we will grasp only the thing that is perfectly light: "Therefore be ye also ready, for in an hour that ye think not, the Son of Man cometh" (Matt. xxiv:44). As to the doctrine of the Kingdom of God or the Kingdom of Heaven, it is not necessary for us to mould it into a perfect theological uniformity in order to enter into the pure, simple New Testament teaching of our Lord's Return. The phrase, "the Kingdom of God," or as it is in the identical passages in Matthew, "the Kingdom of Heaven," is used in half a dozen different significances: it may mean (1) a present, spiritual order; (2) the Church; (3) the service of Christ; (4) the promised Kingdom of the Messiah; (5) God's government of the world; (6) Christ's presence; (7) a future reign of God on the earth; (8) a future Kingdom of the elect. We are not to identify our Lord's Second Coming with any one of these in any way that will weaken the reality and power of the hope and expectancy of His coming in our daily Christian life and experience. As Dr. Mullins says: "The kingdom comes in three senses. It comes in its beginning. It comes in its progress. It comes in its consummation. These are one in principle. The consummation is latent in the beginning. The beginning is patent in the consummation. Jesus beholds the consummation in any event whether at the beginning, in the progress, or at the end. So also the Second Coming of Christ. It is the equivalent of the coming of the kingdom. He comes in the beginning, in the continuance, and in the end of the era. Events belonging to the series which is unified around the Second Coming are in a real sense comings of the Lord. There is a striking saying of Jesus which shows the truth of this last statement. Jesus, in Matthew xxvi:64, says in reply to the high priest's question, 'Henceforth ye shall see the Son of Man sitting at the right hand of power, and coming on the clouds of heaven.' The phrase translated 'henceforth' (*ap' arti*) does not mean 'hereafter,' as if some future time were in view. It means from the time when Jesus spoke the words—'from now on,' He means that the era of God's power, as exerted in and through his Son, has begun. The Son of Man is 'henceforth' the ruler of history."

Now what is our attitude to be during the remainder of our lives toward this hope of Christ's coming? Are we going on indifferent toward it? Will we say, "This is just another of the doctrines that some zealous people tear out of their spiritual significance. I do not believe in any such literalistic idea as that Jesus is coming back again"? Well, the exegesis that spiritualizes away the doctrine of the personal return of Christ imperils the whole Gospel.[5] That is what many people say about His first coming. They will not believe that God was made flesh and dwelt among men. There is a better attitude than that to take towards Christ's coming. I heard of a minister who preached a sermon once in which he said, "I hate that doctrine, that Christ will come back again." That is not the attitude that Paul took toward it, when he wrote to Timothy, "I have finished my course, I have kept the faith: henceforth there is laid up for me a crown of righteousness, which the Lord, the righteous judge, shall give me at that day: and not unto me only, but unto all them also that love His appearing." It is not the attitude that Jesus told us to take toward His coming. He entreated us, if we loved Him, to let our hearts be on the latch for His return: "In the evening, or at midnight, or at the cockcrowing, or in the morning, I will come. What I say unto you, I say unto all; watch. Watch, therefore, lest when the Son of Man cometh, He shall find you sleeping." Have we been watching for Him? Are we watching for Him now? Will we be watching for Him this evening as we lie down to rest, knowing that

---

[5] "Objections cannot be opposed to this doctrine other than such as bear equally against special revelation, creation, divine providence or the incarnation."—(E. J. Wolf in *Lectures on the Augsburg Confession*, First Series, 1866–86, p. 635.)

though He tarry He will return? If we love Him, can our attitude be other than the longing with which the Bible ends, "Even so, come, Lord Jesus"?

"It may be in the evening,
When the work of the day is done,
And you have time to sit in the twilight
And watch the sinking sun,
While the long, bright day dies slowly
Over the sea,
And the hour grows quiet and holy
With thoughts of Me;
While you hear the village children
Passing along the street,
Among those thronging foosteps
May come the sound of My feet.
Therefore, I tell you, Watch,
By the light of the evening star,
When the room is growing dusky
As the clouds afar;
Let the door be on the latch
In your home,
For it may be through the gloaming
I will come.

"It may be when the midnight
Is heavy upon the land
And the black waves lying dumbly
Along the sand;
When the moonless night draws close,
And the lights are out in the house;
When the fire burns low and red,
And the watch is ticking loudly
Beside the bed.
Though you sleep, tired out, on your couch,
Still your heart must wake and watch
In the dark room,
For it may be that at midnight
I will come.

"It may be at the cock-crow,
When the night is dying slowly
In the sky,
And the sea looks calm and holy,
Waiting for the dawn
Of the golden sun,
Which draweth nigh;
When the mists are on the valleys, shading
The rivers chill,
And My morning-star is fading, fading
Over the hill:
Behold, I say unto you, Watch;
Let the door be on the latch
In your home;
In the chill before the dawning,
Between the night and morning,
I may come.

"It may be in the morning,
When the sun is bright and strong,
And the dew is glittering sharply
Over the little lawn;
When the waves are laughing loudly
Along the shore,
And the little birds are singing sweetly
About the door;
With the long day's work before you,
You rise up with the sun,
And the neighbours come in to talk a little
Of all that must be done;
But remember that I may be the next
To come in at the door,
To call you from all your busy work
Forever more.
As you work your heart must watch.
For the door is on the latch
In your room,
And it may be in the morning
I will come."

So He passed down my cottage garden,
By the path that leads to the sea,
Till He came to the turn of the little road
Where the birch and laburnum tree
Lean over and arch the way;
There I saw Him a moment stay,
And turn once more to me,
As I wept at the cottage door,
And lift up His hands in blessing—
Then I saw His face no more.

And I stood still in the doorway,
Leaning against the wall,
Not heeding the fair white roses,
Though I crushed them and let them fall;
Only looking down the pathway,
And looking towards the sea,
And wondering, and wondering
When He would come back for me,
Till I was aware of an angel
Who was going swiftly by,
With the gladness of one who goeth
In the light of God most high.

He passed the end of the cottage
Towards the garden gate,—
(I suppose he was come down
At the setting of the sun
To comfort someone in the village
Whose dwelling was desolate),
And he paused before the door
Beside my place,
And the likeness of a smile
Was on his face:—
"Weep not," he said, "for unto you is given
To watch for the coming of His feet
Who is the Glory of our blessed heaven.
The work and watching will be very sweet,
Even in an earthly home,
And in such an hour as you think not,
He will come."

So I am watching quietly
Every day.
Whenever the sun shines brightly,
I rise and say,
"Surely it is the shining of His face,"
And look unto the gates of His high place
Beyond the sea,
For I know He is coming shortly
To summon me.

And when a shadow falls across the window
Of my room,
Where I am working my appointed task,
I lift my head to watch the door, and ask
If He is come;
And the Angel answers sweetly,
In my home,
"Only a few more shadows,
And He will come." [6]

[6] Barbara MacAndrew, *Ezekiel and Other Poems.*

INDEX

Printed in the United States of America